C000174352

METRO-CAMMELL
150 years of craftsmanship

KEITH BEDDOES, COLIN AND STEPHEN WHEELER

This 8 plank 15 ton coal wagon of 1908 was part of the private owner fleet of Metropolitan Amalgamated.
Historical Model Railway Society

RUNPAST PUBLISHING

SOME COMPANY PATENTS, INNOVATIONS & ORIGINAL DEVELOPMENTS

1835	Faggotted axle of forged iron invented	Patent Shaft and Axletree Co
1844	Design patented for coaches mounted on bogies	Joseph Wright & Co
1877	Development of pressed steel underframes and bogies which later influenced motor car chassis design	Leeds Forge
1893	First all-steel coach structure developed	Metropolitan R.C. & W. Co
1920	Patents taken out for self-discharge wagons	Leeds Forge
1924	First suburban EMU stock developed for India	Metropolitan C.W & F. Co
1930	Development of all-metal structure 'bus body and patents taken out for pillar section	Metropolitan Cammell
1933	Trolleybus roof gantries patented	Metropolitan Cammell
1939	Designed first 'chassis-less' trolleybus	Metropolitan Cammell
1946	Royal Train for South African tour designed, developed and completed in a record 9 months	Metropolitan Cammell
1948	First integral 'bus (Olympic) developed	Metropolitan Cammell
1948	First large scale application of aluminium alloy construction in railway passenger stock	Metropolitan Cammell
1965	Development of first 90-ton followed by 100-ton GLW bogie rail tank wagons	Metropolitan Cammell
1968	Automatic trains for London Underground	Metropolitan Cammell

© **K. Beddoes, C. Wheeler, S. Wheeler and Runpast Publishing, November 1999**

All rights reserved. Except for the quotation of brief passages for the purposes of review, no part of this book may be reproduced, stored in a retrieval system, or transmitted in any form or by any means, electronic, mechanical, photocopying, recording or otherwise, without the prior permission of the publisher and copyright owners.

ISBN 1 870754 46 8

Typesetting and reproduction by Viners Wood Associates, Painswick, Glos.
Printed by The Amadeus Press Ltd, Huddersfield.

Introduction

The origins of Metro-Cammell can be traced back to the stage coaches which provided passenger and mail services between London and the provincial cities in the early part of the nineteenth century.

Joseph Wright, a third generation London coachbuilder, was a contractor for the Royal Mails and the owner of most stage coaches then running between London and Birmingham.

Two London addresses are quoted for his firm:- Goswell Road, Clerkenwell and Gough Street, Grays Inn, of which one was probably his carriage works and the other the operating base.

Earlier than most, Joseph Wright foresaw that the new railways being opened in the 1830s would eventually replace the stage coach and with it his livelihood, so seizing the opportunity of being part of this new form of transport he diverted his energies to the manufacture of railway carriages in his London works using the skills and experience of the coach builders already employed by him.

Precisely in which year Joseph Wright first made railway carriages is not clear but from January 1838 he is known to have owned and leased the entire stock of 56 passenger coaches of the London and Greenwich Railway, London's first railway, which had opened in December 1836. In August 1837 he accepted an order from the London and Southampton Railway for twelve first class, twelve second class, twelve third class and six excursion coaches followed by a second, similar, order. All were four-wheeled, the first class resembling three stage coach bodies mounted on a common underframe. Joseph Wright also contracted to supply coaches to the London and Birmingham Railway which opened in 1838 and soon attracted traffic away from his stage coaches on the London to Birmingham road.

By 1842 several railways were radiating out from Birmingham, forming a network of connecting lines from the Midlands to other commercial areas of the country, and one of these, the newly formed Midland Railway, sent six first-class carriages to Joseph Wright for repair in 1844. As trade grew so did a demand for more rolling stock, so Joseph Wright decided to move his carriage works from London to an area near Birmingham with more room to expand.

The chosen site was alongside the Birmingham and Derby Junction Railway, as this location, with a rail connection, would give direct access for incoming raw materials whilst delivery of the finished product would be cheaper and quicker, plus many of the nearby Birmingham metalworking trades could be drawn upon to supply tools, components and fittings.

Six acres of meadow land was acquired in April 1845, at Saltley, then just an olde world village and very soon construction work began.

In the summer of 1845 the works were so complete that carriage building began in a factory described then as containing 'the newest and most expeditious mechanical appliances' and consisted of 'workshops, offices, a wharf and other buildings' and included 'engines, boilers and other machinery'.

From those early beginnings, this book follows over 150 years of rolling stock manufacture in the West Midlands by a company that arguably reshaped the rolling stock industry despite two world wars, recession, name changes and mergers.

It is not the definitive story, however, it is an ongoing one, for just a mile away from Joseph Wright's original site (in use today for other purposes) Alstom Transport Ltd in its Midland works at Washwood Heath still carries on the tradition of Britain's leading rail vehicle manufacturer, hopefully well into the twenty-first century.

Acknowledgements

Many people, too numerous to mention, gave help, advice and information in this book's preparation for which we offer our gratitude, but particular thanks are due to the following:

The late John H Price for the use of his original notes and information
Alstom Transport Ltd including Mrs J Rogers (Sales and Marketing) and I C Castledine & N Hughes
George Behrend (Wagon Lits Society)
Bob Heron (Wagon Lits Society)
Terry Bye (Pullman Society)
John Watkins
Brian J R Yates
Garry Yates
Roy Humphries
William Murphy
Jorge L San-Martin (Argentina)
A Brown
Birmingham Reference Library
John Edgington
The Tank Museum
Historical Model Railway Society
Jack Slinn
Mrs S Beddoes for editing the manuscript
Mrs C Taylor for coping with the typing
Stephen Mourton, our publisher, for researching additional information

Unless otherwise credited all the photographs are from the private collections of Colin and Stephen Wheeler, John Watkins and Brian J R Yates.

Contents

100 *years of* *Craftsmanship*

1845 to 1945

Rich in tradition and superb in craftsmanship—from the building of a State Coach for H.H. The Viceroy of Egypt nearly 100 years ago—to the production of the latest fully air-conditioned Saloons for the South African Railways—the name METROPOLITAN-CAMMELL represents generations of skill backed by modern technique and stands supreme.

METROPOLITAN-CAMMELL
CARRIAGE & WAGON Co LIMITED

SUBSIDIARY AND CONTROLLED COMPANIES
THE MIDLAND RAILWAY-CARRIAGE & WAGON Co., Ltd.
THE LEEDS FORGE Co., Ltd.   THE PATENT SHAFT & AXLETREE Co., Ltd.
Head Office: SALTLEY. BIRMINGHAM.   London Office: VICKERS HOUSE, BROADWAY, WESTMINSTER, S.W.1.

Rolling stock manufacturers were regular advertisers in trade publications such as *The Locomotive Magazine, Railway Gazette – A Journal of Management, Engineering and Operation, Railway Engineer, Modern Transport* and early editions of *Railway Magazine*. Metro-Cammell used this advertisement in *The Railway Gazette* to celebrate its centenary, 1845 to 1945. Interestingly, a much earlier advert, from a 1902 *Railway Magazine*, reproduced on page nine, claims the firm was established in 1835. This may refer to the date that Joseph Wright started manufacturing railway carriages at his London premises, as the firm was well established in the market before it started building at Saltley in 1845.

What would nowadays be called a press release was used to announce details of new vehicles. With luck, a magazine would reproduce not just a picture of the vehicle, but also its specification, giving the builder valuable exposure. Such an example is the article on the 3ft gauge first class carriage built for the West Clare Railway in Ireland, which appeared in *The Locomotive* magazine in October 1902 and is reproduced on page eleven.

CHAPTER 1

Joseph Wright and Sons 1845-1862

Joseph Wright's Railway Carriage & Wagon Works at Saltley was a success from the start, despite the emergence of competition. A London connection was still retained, but only an office at 8 Adam Street, Adelphi, for after becoming established at Saltley the London works were disposed of.

It is interesting to note that in the firm's early advertisements the Royal Crest was displayed which no doubt Joseph Wright had title to as the builder of the Royal Mail coaches at the former London works.

In 1847 a further 42 acres of adjacent meadow land at Saltley was taken on lease for future expansion and as new shops were constantly erected on this land to form a new works in 1853, the original 1845 buildings were then leased to the London and North Western Railway for carriage building until its own carriage works was ready at Wolverton. Wright's new plant included two large finishing and painting shops capable of taking 50 to 60 vehicles. As the works prospered and grew so did the village of Saltley and this was a major influence behind the opening of a station there by the Midland Railway on 1 October 1854.

By 1858 the works employed 1300 men, though this fell again to 700 in 1886 as the major British railway companies set up their own carriage and wagon works, leaving the private builders increasingly dependent on exports. Fortunately, many developing railways overseas were British-engineered and British-run, and their promoters turned to home industry for their rolling stock. One firm, the Birmingham Railway Carriage & Wagon Co Ltd at Smethwick (BRCW), for many years functioned mainly as a supplier to the British-owned railway companies in Argentine with whom it shared some directors.

Joseph Wright died in 1859, and the business was continued by his sons, Henry and Joseph, under the same name. New capital was now needed so when the Companies Act of 1862 became law, Joseph Wright and Sons was registered in March 1862 as a limited liability company; The Metropolitan Railway Carriage & Wagon Company Limited; the name presumably chosen to reflect the company's London origins. The initial nominal capital was £100,000, which allowed the company to buy the whole undertaking except for the Old Works which remained occupied by the London & North Western Railway until 1870, when the Metropolitan Company purchased the unexpired leasehold, so becoming the owners of Wright's original works. In 1864 the share capital was increased to £200,000, one reason for the increase was to finance the supply of carriages and wagons (especially mineral wagons) on hire purchase, or for lease, which become a particular feature of British wagon-building. The wagons usually bore the name of a colliery company, but closer examination would reveal the works plate of one of the wagon-finance companies associated with a wagon-builder. The leased wagons would be the subject of a maintenance contract, and Metropolitan maintained wagon repair facilities at various places where empty coal wagons would congregate.

All the vehicles produced before 1862 were four or six wheelers, but Joseph Wright had taken out a Patent (No 10173 of 1844) for carriages with four, six or eight-wheeled bogies. Special types included a saloon carriage for the Khedive of Egypt, part of a royal train, described years later as looking like an ambitious summer-house in a suburban garden. No complete list of Joseph Wright's customers is known to survive, but a partial list has been compiled from the register of microfiche drawings held by the Birmingham Central Reference Library.

Orders placed with Joseph Wright in the winter of 1861-2 were completed by the Metropolitan Company (see list).

Joseph Wright & Sons
Known rolling stock customers 1845 to 1862

British and Irish Railways

Belfast & County Down	
Blyth & Tyne	Londonderry
Dublin & Meath	Newry Warrenpoint & Rostrevor
Chester & Birkenhead	North Staffordshire
Eastern Counties	Norwich & Brandon
Edinburgh & Glasgow	Oswestry & Newtown
Great Southern & Western	Portpatrick
Great Western	St Helens
Hereford Hay & Brecon	Scottish Central
Leven & East of Fife	Seaham Harbour
London & Birmingham	Seaham & Sunderland
London & North Western	Shrewsbury & Chester
London & South Western	South Eastern
London Brighton & South Coast	Ulster Railway
London Chatham & Dover	Waterford & Limerick

Overseas Railways

Adelaide & Gawler	Melbourne & Hobsons Bay
Barcelona & Granollers	New South Wales Government
Coquimbo (Chile)	Paraguay
Danube & Black Sea	Royal Danish
Egyptian Royal Train	Royal Swedish
Egyptian State	Stephenson Clarke (contractor)
Great Indian Peninsular	Tijuca (Brazil)
Jamaica	Victorian Railways
Kongsvinger (Norway)	

Above: A very early 1st class coach built by Joseph Wright, Saltley, for the Shrewsbury and Chester Railway in 1846. Seen here as GWR pilot van No.22, withdrawn in August 1874. The road stage coach influence prevailed for some time in early rolling stock design.   *G.W.R.*

Below: Ex Chester & Birkenhead coach built by Joseph Wright, Saltley in 1854. Seen here as GWR 1st No.719, withdrawn in June 1882. 18' 1" long, 7' 5" wide, wheelbase 10'. Weight empty 5T 12.5cwt.   *G.W.R.*

Above: Composite coach built in 1856 by Joseph Wright, Saltley. Became West Midland Railway No.134, then GWR No.214 in 1863 and GWR No.742 in 1873.

G.W.R.

Below: GWR first/second composite coach No.319, built by Metropolitan Railway Carriage & Wagon Company, Saltley, June 1867.

G.W.R.

Midland Railway No.528 was one of a batch of 29' slip carriages built by Metropolitan in 1874. Slip carriages were detached from a train while in motion and were used to serve stations where the main train did not stop. They were usually brought to a stand at the platform by hand brake only.

Kidderminster Railway Museum

CHAPTER 2

Metropolitan Railway Carriage and Wagon Company Ltd 1863-1901

In its early years, Metropolitan received useful orders from the Midland Railway, supplying 150 composite coaches in 1863 and 1864. In 1866 Metropolitan successfully tendered to build 20 first-class carriages for the Midland; they were 20' long, with three compartments, and were supplied without wheels and springs, which were added by the Midland's Derby Works. Metropolitan obtained another order that year for composite carriages while other business followed over the next few years including repair work and, in 1872, construction of 35 third-class carriages and sixty composites, all still 4-wheelers. By way of contrast, the mid-1870s saw Metropolitan build 32 12-wheeler bogie carriages, the first of that wheel arrangement and said to be the best ordinary coaches on any British railway. Twenty of these were intended for use on the Midland's new Settle-Carlisle line, although it is recorded in *Midland Railway Carriages, Volume 1*, that railway carriage builders were having great difficulty fulfilling all the orders placed with them and none had been delivered by Metropolitan by the line's opening date for passenger traffic, May Day 1876.

Orders from the big railways reduced dramatically as they became virtually self-sufficient but there were still many smaller independent lines in the British Isles in the late nineteenth century which relied on outside manufacturers. One was the Swindon, Marlborough and Andover Railway which ordered its opening stock in 1881 from Metropolitan. This included five 6-wheeled composite carriages; two 4-wheeled brake/thirds; two horseboxes; fifteen cattle wagons; twenty-three open wagons; ten covered vans; two brake vans; and two trucks for the conveyance of road carriages. Being somewhat impoverished, the SMAR resorted to hire purchase for the acquisition from Metropolitan of twelve carriages in 1882, plus four horseboxes and twenty-five open wagons in 1883. The SMAR was absorbed into the Midland & South Western Junction Railway which eventually operated from Cheltenham to Andover and Southampton and orders dried up as the MSWJ had financial problems. New management and funding for the railway in the 1890s provided worthwhile orders for Metropolitan's then competitors, the Oldbury Railway Carriage Co and the Midland Railway Carriage & Wagon Co, Shrewsbury. Bogie carriages, more horseboxes, cattle wagons and covered wagons were among the new stock supplied by these companies, which themselves subsequently became part of the Metropolitan company. Later in its independent existence the MSWJ acquired carriages and other stock second-hand from the Midland Railway.

The late Victorian years included some periods of slack trade, when demand for carriages and wagons slumped and much of the hire fleet stood idle. Part of Metropolitan's response was to diversify into building tramcars. Names of 35 horse, steam and cable tramways appear in the register of drawings, but there were certainly more, especially for export.

The passing of the Tramways Act in 1870 marked the start of horse tramway expansion in Britain. Prior to 1870 Britain had only one specialist tram builder (George Starbuck of Birkenhead) and the excess demand was met by imports from John Stephenson of New York, plus a few from Denmark. Metropolitan saw its chance and in 1870 built a sample car as a demonstrator. It was an enlarged version of the Starbuck type of two-horse double-decker with back-to-back 'knifeboard' seating outside. Other types were soon added, such as smaller double-deckers of 1872 to work between Birmingham and West Bromwich, and some one-horse single-deckers. The first large order was 70 cars for Dublin. A drawing exists of an 1876 batch for Dublin: these cost £194 each, weighed 2.5 tons, and seated 20 passengers inside and 22 outside. They were built in oak and ash with mahogany panels, and their axlebox springing was provided by rubber blocks in compression. A similar car of 1883, but with improved stairs, was used on the Fintona Tramway until 1957 and is preserved in the Belfast Transport Museum.

Metropolitan built the two cars of Britain's first seaside funicular, the Scarborough South Cliff Tramway, which opened on 6 July 1875. The main contractor was Crossley Brothers Ltd of Manchester, whose gas engines were used to pump sea-water

METROPOLITAN RAILWAY CARRIAGE AND WAGON COMPANY, LIMITED,

(Successors to Messrs. JOSEPH WRIGHT & SONS.)

Designers & Constructors of...

RAILWAY CARRIAGES & WAGONS, TRAM-CARS, IRONWORK for the same of ENGLISH, AMERICAN and all other Types. ROLLING STOCK of all kinds supplied for Cash or upon deferred payment.

WAGONS LET UPON SIMPLE HIRE. . .

ESTABLISHED 1835.

Offices : SALTLEY WORKS, BIRMINGHAM.

No.643 is one of the thirty-two magnificent 54' composite, 6-wheel bogie carriages built by Metropolitan for the Midland Railway, to the design of T.G. Clayton, the Midland's Carriage and Wagon Superintendent. Such vehicles earned the Midland an enviable reputation for the best in passenger comfort. Twelve carriages to this design were also built by the Ashbury company.

Kidderminster Railway Museum

to the lift head for use as water-ballast. Saltley Works also built the cars of the 1884 cliff tramway at Saltburn. At the time of writing, both these lines are still at work, with re-bodied cars.

Metropolitan's share of the market for steam tram trailers was higher than for horse trams. The Board of Trade would only allow each steam tram engine to draw one car, and this caused the companies to use large double-deck cars mounted on bogies and built on steel underframes. The first such drawings are dated 1880 and 1881, and the first orders were completed in 1882/3. Saltley Works also built the 1887 cars of the street-running Edinburgh Northern cable tramway, as sub-contractors to Dick, Kerr and Co.

The destination of vehicles shipped overseas can often be difficult to trace, especially when ordered through agents, so when members of the British Association visited Saltley Works in August 1886, they saw some Lilliputian-size vehicles for a 2ft gauge tramway in Western Australia and it was not until 1974 that the customer was positively identified as the Roebourne-Cossack horse tramway, built in 1887 to serve the West Pilbara goldfield some 1200 miles north of Perth. It was closed in 1926 after cyclone damage and replaced by a 3ft 6in gauge railway, part of which survives to serve a turtle soup factory!

Another strange tale concerns Lord Kitchener's saloon, one of two vehicles built by Metropolitan in 1885 for the proposed Suakin-Berber military railway from the Red Sea to the Nile Valley. Only twenty of the planned 322 route miles were completed, further progress being thwarted by raiding tribesmen who stole the rails and telegraph wire and set fire to the sleepers. The project was abandoned in April 1886 and twenty ships still loaded with railway material were ordered back to England. Some was used for a military railway at Lydd and for coastal defence work at Sandgate, whilst the saloon coach was used on the military railway at Shoeburyness until transferred in 1990 to the Museum of Army Transport at Beverley. The saloon was never used by Lord Kitchener, and probably never placed on rails in the Sudan.

The list of customers to whom the Metropolitan Railway Carriage & Wagon Co Ltd supplied railway rolling stock between 1863 and 1901 reads like a directory of the world's railways. All five continents were represented, featuring ten companies in America, six in Africa, seven in Asia, two in Australasia and fourteen in Europe. The largest number of separate customers was in England (36), followed by Ireland (17), Wales (14) and the Argentine (11).

It is interesting to note rolling stock delivered to those English railways that were built to the GWR 7ft broad gauge.

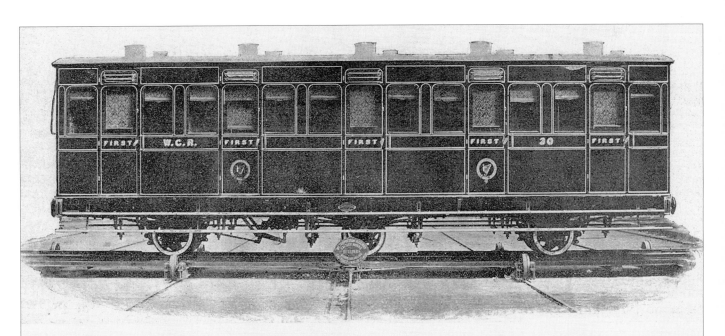

FIRST CLASS CARRIAGE, WEST CLARE RAILWAY.

———//———

THIS carriage is 30-ft. 10 in. long, 6 ft. 6-in. wide outside dimensions, and 6-ft. 8-in. high from floor to roof in centre inside, divided into five compartments, mounted on three pairs of wheels 2-ft. 1-in. diameter, each pair 9-ft. 9-in. apart centres. The body is constructed of Moulmein teak and the underframe of North American white oak, the solebars having iron plates ¼-in. thick on the outsides.

The interior has spring cushions to the seats and backs, stuffed with curled horsehair and covered with moquette. The roof and backs above the trimming are lined with lincrusta, finished with mahogany banding. Each window is provided with a patent adjustable tapestry blind. The carriage is fitted with the automatic vacuum brake, combined central buffers and drawbars, and axleboxes for oil lubrication. The gauge of the line is 3-ft.

The Metropolitan Railway Carriage and Wagon Co., Ltd., are the builders, to whom we are indebted for the above particulars. Mr. Geo. Hopkins, the locomotive superintendent of the W. C. Ry., is the designer.

The Metropolitan Railway Carriage & Wagon Co Ltd – Railway Customers 1863 to 1901

British and Irish Railways

Aberdare
Ballycastle
Barry Dock
Belfast & County Down
Belfast & Northern Counties
Blyth & Tyne
Brecon & Merthyr
Bristol & Exeter   (BG)
Bristol Port & Pier   (BG)
Caledonian
Cambrian
Cavan & Leitrim
Cheshire Lines
Clogher Valley
Colne Valley
Cork & Muskerry
Cork Blackrock & Passage
Corris
Deeside
Dublin & South Eastern

Dublin Wicklow & Wexford
Great Eastern
Great North of Scotland
Great Northern
Great Northern (Ireland)
Great Southern & Western (Ireland)
Great Western
Hereford Hay & Brecon
Hull & Barnsley
Isle of Man
Isle of Wight
Jersey
Lambourn Valley
Lancashire Derbyshire & East Coast
Lancashire & Yorkshire
Leven & East of Fife
Liskeard & Caradon   (BG)
London Brighton & South Coast
London Chatham & Dover
London Tilbury & Southend

Londonderry & Lough Swilly
Manchester & Milford
Manchester Sheffield &
   Lincolnshire
Maryport & Carlisle
Mawddwy
Metropolitan
Mid-Wales
Midland
Midland & South Western Junction
Newry & Armagh
Newry Warrenpoint & Rostrevor
North British
North Eastern
North London
North Staffordshire
North Wales Narrow Gauge
Port Talbot Railway & Works Co
Rhymney
Royal Albert Dock

T Savin (contractor)
Scottish Central
Seaham Harbour
Sirhowy
Somerset & Dorset
South Devon   (BG)
South Eastern
W Stableford (contractor)
Swindon Marlborough & Andover
Taff Vale
Teesside
Thetford & Watton
Waterford & Limerick
Waterford & Central Ireland
Waterford Dungarvan & Lismore
Waterford & Tramore
West Lancashire
Whitehaven Cleator & Egremont

(BG) = Broad Gauge

Known Overseas Railway Customers

Alcoy and Gandia
Andino (Argentine)
Argentine Great Western
Argentine North Eastern
Athens & Piraeus (Royal Saloon)
Auckland & Drury (N Z)
Bahia Blanca North Western
Bahia & Sao Fransisco (Brazil)
Bellavista & San Roque (Argentina)
Bombay & Baroda
Buenos Aires Northern
Buenos Aires & Pacific
Buenos Aires & Rosario
Cape Government
Central Argentine
Central of Brazil
Central Uruguay
Cerro de Pasco (Peru)
Columbo Harbour
Coquimbo (Chile)

Danube & Black Sea
Delhi
Demarara (Guiana)
Deniliquin & Moana (Australia)
Enrique Cortes(contractor)
Egyptian State
Great Indian Peninsula
Great Southern of Spain
Howlison (contractor)
Imperial Chinese
Imperial Japanese
Jamaica Government
Jaraslav-Vologda (Russia)
Kiushu (Japan)
Leopoldina (Brazil)
Malta
Manila & Dagupan
Mauritius
Melbourne & Hobsons Bay
Mysore State

National Railway of Tehuantepec
   (Mexico)
Natal Government
New South Wales Government
New Zealand Government
Nizam of Hyderabad
Norwegian Trunk
Oudh & Rohilkund
Paulista (Brazil)
Perak (Malaya)
Portuguese Governors Saloon
   (E Africa)
Royal Sardinian
Royal Swedish
Russian Government
Santander-Lierganes
Sanyo (Japan)
Sao Paulo (Brazil)
Scinde (India)
Selandor (Malaya)

Singapore-Johore
South East Portugal
Southern Nigerian
South Indian
Suakim-Berber (see text)
Sungei Ujong (Malaya)
Tarkwa (Gold Coast)
Taltal (Chile)
Tasmania
Tharsis (Spain)
Tongoy (Chile)
Transandino
Trinidad Government
Uganda
Uruguay del Este
Valparaiso-Santiago
Venezuela
Villa Maria-Rufino (Argentine)
West of India Portugese Guaranteed
West Australian Government

Known Tramway Customers

J Aird (contractor)
Admiralty (Haslar Hospital, Gosport)
Birmingham & Aston
Birmingham & District
Birmingham & Midland
Birmingham Tramways Co
Cavehill & Whitewell, Belfast
Dublin Tramways
Edinburgh & District
Edinburgh Northern
Mr Felts (for pier tramway)
Fintona (Ireland)
Fisher & Parrish (contractor)

Glasgow Corporation
Glasgow Street Tramways
Johannesburg City & Suburban
Kreeft Howard (contractor)
North Dublin
North London Suburban
North Staffordshire
Oxford & Aylesbury
Peak Tramway (Hong Kong)
P W Pearson (contractor)
Pernambuco
Phillips & Co. (contractors)
Portstewart

Saltburn Cliff Lift
Scarborough Cliff Lift
Siam
Singapore
South Shields
South Staffordshire
Southwark & Deptford
Stockton & Darlington
Taite & Carlton (contractors)
Trinidad Tramway
Tripoli (Lebanon)
Tynemouth
Universal Steam Tramway Co

Vale of Clyde
West Australian Government
J Whittall (contractor)
F C Winby (contractor)
R Whyte (contractor)
Woolwich & South East London

The register of drawings includes
a further 40 horse and steam
trams and 3 funicular cars without
naming the customers

CHAPTER 3

Amalgamation 1902

The year 1900 may conveniently be taken as the peak of railway carriage and wagon building by private firms in Britain. Until that time, there was enough profitable work for most of the time for everyone in the trade, and Britain could claim to have two-thirds of the world's passenger coach trade. After 1900, a gradual decline set in, almost imperceptibly at first, as overseas countries (and those British railway companies not already equipped) began to establish their own rolling stock manufacturing facilities. Britain still supplied wheels, axles, underframes and bogies, as well as the more complex vehicles such as sleeping and dining cars and saloons, but there would be fewer orders for ordinary wagons and coaches.

Industrial history provides many cases where over-capacity and a fall in demand brought a drop in prices and drove the weaker firms out of business. The UK carriage and wagon firms managed in general to match capacity to demand and avoid price cutting or other adverse consequences. That they did so was due in large measure to the farsightedness of Frank Dudley Docker of Edgbaston. Dudley Docker was Chairman of the Patent Shaft Co and a director and co-founder of Docker Brothers, paint and varnish manufacturers to the various rolling stock builders, with whom he developed close contacts, and he became convinced that there would be major advantages in making mergers and agreements within the rolling stock industry.

Docker worked out his plan and put it to the various companies during 1901. Some agreed to join, others would co-operate, but preferred to remain (outwardly) independent. The anticipated savings would come from specialisation between factories, economy in tendering and advertising, bulk purchasing and the ability to execute contracts too large for any one works. It was a bold plan and it succeeded.

To effect the merger, a new company, the Metropolitan Amalgamated Railway Carriage & Wagon Co Ltd, headed by Dudley Docker, was registered on 18 April 1902. The participating companies were the Ashbury Railway Carriage & Iron Co Ltd, Openshaw; the Lancaster Railway Carriage & Wagon Co Ltd, Lancaster; Brown, Marshalls & Co Ltd, Saltley; The Metropolitan Railway Carriage & Wagon Co Ltd, Saltley; and the Oldbury Railway Carriage & Wagon Co Ltd, Oldbury. Subsequent acquisitions were the Patent Shaft & Axletree Co Ltd, Wednesbury; Docker Brothers Ltd, the Willingsworth Iron & Steel Co. and the works of George F Milnes & Co Ltd, at Hadley near Wellington, Shropshire.

The latter situation arose in 1904 in tramcar building, with the failure of George F Milnes Castle Car Works, Hadley and the British Electric Car Co Ltd of Trafford Park, Manchester. These events were closely watched by the Metropolitan group, and fearing that a buyer might use them to build railway vehicles, in competition, Dudley Docker together with directors of The British Electric Car Co. and Dick, Kerr & Co., formed the Castle Car Syndicate Ltd in December 1904 to buy the two factories. However shortly after this move a Dick, Kerr subsidiary, The Electric Railway & Tramway Carriage Works Co. was renamed United Electric Car Co., which then purchased from the syndicate, both the Trafford Park Works of British Electric Car Co., and George Milnes of Hadley early in 1905. United Electric then leased the Hadley works, from its re-opening in July 1905, to Metropolitan Amalgamated for building wagons and carriages.

In April 1907 Metropolitan Amalgamated acquired the whole site but in 1908 falling orders forced them to close it, some employees transferring to the Birmingham plants. In the three years that Metropolitan Amalgamated operated the Hadley factory, 1036 wagons and 133 carriages were built. In 1910 Joseph Sankey & Sons Ltd of Bilston bought the works, and their successors, GKN Sankey Ltd still occupy the much enlarged factory at Hadley, now part of Telford.

At their maximum extent (1905 to 1907) the factories of Metropolitan Amalgamated employed 14,000 men and occupied no less than 599 acres – Saltley 48, Britannia (ex Brown and Marshalls) 11, Oldbury 20, Ashbury 20, Lancaster 15, Hadley 10 and Wednesbury Steelworks 475.

Rolling stock built for overseas railways was usually the result of various collaborative efforts. Sometimes a railway designed its own stock: other times it would present a general specification to the manufacturer, or it engaged a firm of consulting engineers who would draw up a detailed design and supervise the whole project for its customer. Names of consulting firms which crop up time and again in the history of British rolling stock construction include *Rendel, Palmer and Tritton*; *Livesay, Son and Henderson*; *Sir Douglas Fox and Partners*; *Sir John Wolfe Barry & Partners*; while the Crown Agents for the Colonies were often employed.

Many sub-contractors were also involved with the main manufacturer and a glance through trade publications shows advertisements from various suppliers, often based in the traditional 'metal bashing' areas of Birmingham and the 'Black Country', so handily placed to supply the local rolling stock builders with their requirements for everything from split pins to the finest bathroom fittings.

Above: GWR second class coach No.385 (ex No.25) 19' 8" long, 7' 5" wide. Built by Ashbury Carriage Company in July 1857.

G.W.R.

Below: 4 wheel composite coach built by the Railway Carriage Company, Oldbury in June 1869. It is seen here on the Golden Valley Railway, Herefordshire in the opening years of this century carrying GWR No.418. It was condemned in March 1905.

W.H. Smith

Principal Known Customers of Merged Companies, 1846 to 1901

Ashbury Railway Carriage & Iron Co Ltd

BRITISH AND IRISH RAILWAYS

Belfast & County Down, Belfast & Northern Counties, Central London, City & South London , Cork & Macroom, Cork & Youghal, Dublin & Drogheda, Dublin & South Eastern, East Lancashire, Ebbw Vale, Furness, Great Central, Great Northern (Ireland), Great Southern & Western (Ireland), Great Western, Irish North Western, Isle of Man, Liverpool & Manchester, Manchester & Leeds, Manchester Sheffield & Lincolnshire, Mersey, Metropolitan, Midland, Midland & Great Western, Sligo Leitrim & Northern Counties, Waterford Limerick & Western, Waterford & Tramore, Wirral

OVERSEAS RAILWAYS

Assam-Bengal, Barsi (India), Bergslagens (Sweden), Cape Central, Cape Government, Ceylon Government, Mauritius, Sao Paulo (Brazil), Singapore, South African Field Force, Tasmania, Trinidad, Uganda, W. Australian Government, Zafra-Huelva & Other Railways in Argentina, Brazil, Chile, Egypt, India, Mexico, Peru, Spain, Uruguay, Venezuela

TRAMWAYS

Accrington, Bessbrook & Newry, Blackburn, Bradford, Darwin, Devils Dyke Steep Grade, Dewsbury, Dublin & Lucan, Glyn Valley, Lincoln, Lytham (Gas Trams), Morecambe, Sheffield, Southport Pier, all buyers of Eade's Patent Reversible horse cars,

Carriages built by Ashbury which survive include three ex Metropolitan Railway bogie vehicles on the Bluebell Railway in East Sussex, of which two, built in 1898 and 1900, were restored to service in 1999. A replica of the Ashbury coach used on the Metropolitan Railway's Brill branch has recently been constructed at Quainton Road, Buckinghamshire.

Lancaster Railway Carriage & Wagon Co Ltd

BRITISH AND IRISH RAILWAYS

Cheshire Lines, Colne Valley, Cork Bandon & South Coast, Cork & Macroom, East Coast Joint Stock, Furness, Great Central, Isle of Wight, Lancashire Derbyshire & East Coast, London Brighton & South Coast, London Chatham & Dover, Londonderry & Lough Swilly, Midland, Midland Great Western, Northampton & Banbury Junction, Snowdon Mountain, South Eastern, Sproston & Co (contractor), Talyllyn, Weston Clevedon & Portishead (Argentine export rejects), Whittingham.

OVERSEAS RAILWAYS

Algeciras & Bobadilla, Anglo-Chilian Nitrate, Arauco (Chile), Barsi Light Railway (India), Brazil Great Southern, Buenos Aires Great Southern, Buenos Aires & Ensenada, Buenos Aires & Rosario, Cape Government, Central Argentine, Central South African, Ceylon Government, Columbo Harbour, East Argentine, Egyptian State, Indian State, Itapimirim (Brazil), Junin (Chile), Kerr Stuart (agent), Lima, Mauritius, Madrid & Portugal, Midland of Western Australia, Mexico Southern, Minas & Rio (including Emperor of Brazil's saloon), Mogiana (Brazil), New South Wales Governmen, Nilgiri (India), Russia, Santa Ana (Salvador), Sante Fe and Cordoba, Singapore-Johore, Suakin-Berber, Tarapaca (Peru), Tasmania, Transandino (Argentine), Trinidad, Uganda, Uruguay Midland, Venezuela and other railways in South America, West Australian Government

TRAMWAYS

Blackpool, Bury, Hobart (Tasmania), Lancaster & District, Lancaster Corporation, Lytham, Morecambe, Neath, Rio de Janeiro (Villa Isabel), Ryde Pier, South London, South Staffordshire, Trafford Park. No full list has been found of Lancaster's exports.

The narrow gauge Talyllyn Railway in North Wales has in operation a carriage built in 1870 by Lancaster Railway Carriage & Wagon Co Ltd.

Oldbury Railway Carriage & Wagon Co Ltd

BRITISH AND IRISH RAILWAYS	Ballycastle, Belfast & County Down, County Donegal, Glasgow Subway,	Golden Valley, Great Southern & Western, Great Western, Hull & Barnsley,	Isle of Wight, Londonderry & Lough Swilly, Metropolitan,	Midland & South Western Junction South Eastern & Chatham, Ulster Railway, Woolwich Arsenal.
OVERSEAS RAILWAYS	Bukhtiapur-Bihar (India), Baraset-Basirhat (India), Bikaner State (India),	Burma, Cantagallo (Brazil), Ceylon,	Howrah-Amta-Sheakhala, Indian State, Japan,	Jodhpur-Bikaner, Rhanaghat-Krashnagar, Udaipur-Chitagarh.
TRAMWAYS	Birmingham & Midland,	John Grantham's Steam Car (for Merryweathers & Sons).		No published list has been found for the Oldbury Co.

Brown Marshalls & Co Ltd

| BRITISH AND IRISH RAILWAYS

Ballymena & Larne, Barry, Cheshire Lines, Cork Bandon & South Coast, Dublin & South Eastern,	Festiniog, Finn Valley, Great Eastern, Great Northern (Ireland), Great North of Scotland, Great Western, Highland, Hull & Barnsley, Irish North Western,	Isle of Man, Lambourn Valley, Lancashire Derbyshire & East Coast, Lee-on-the-Solent, Liverpool Overhead, London & Birmingham, London Brighton & South Coast,	Londonderry, London Tilbury & Southend, Metropolitan, Midland, Midland Great Western (Ireland), North Wales Narrow Gauge,	Portland, Rhondda Valley, Rhondda & Swansea Bay, South Eastern, Talyllyn, Ulster Railway, Waterford & Central Ireland, Waterford Limerick & Western.
OVERSEAS RAILWAYS

Adelaide & Glenelg, Agricultural (Egypt), Andino (Argentina), Antofagasta-Salar (Chile), Argentine Great Western, Argentine North Eastern, Argentine Presidential Saloons, Assam-Bengal, Bengal & Nagpur, Bombay Baroda & Central India, Buenos Aires & Ensenada, Buenos Aires Great Southern, | Buenos Aires Mercedes, Buenos Aires Western, Cairo-Helwan, Central Entre Rios, Great Northern Argentine, Central of Brazil, Ceylon Goverment, Chinese Government, Cordoba & North Western, Delagoa Bay & East Africa (Mozambique), Delhi, Demarara (Guiana), Donna Thereza Christina (Brazil), East Indian, Egyptian State, | Gold Coast, Imperial Japanese, Indian Midland, Jamaica, Kena-Aswan, Kyrenia Harbour, Lima (Peru), Majorca, Manila Railway, Martin & Co (India), Mashonaland (Rhodesia), 1888 Melbourne Exhibition, Minas & Rio (Brazil), Natal Government, New Zealand Government, New Zealand Midland, Nizam of Hyderabab, | Oudh & Rohikund, Paraguay Central, Paulista (Brazil), Perak (Malaya), Puerto Cabello & Valencia (Venezuela), Rhodesia, Rohikund & Kumaon, Santa Fe (Argentina), Santiago-Valparaiso, Scotish Australian Mining Co, Selangor (Malaya), Sicilian, South African Replublic, South Australian, Southern Mahratta, Syrian Ottoman, | Tasmania, Tharsis (Spain), Transandino, Trinidad, Uruguay Great Eastern, Uruguay Midland, Victorian, West Australian Government, Western Railway of Buenos Aires, Yarosalv-Vologda (Russia),

Three dining cars for the Calais-Brindisi Peninsular and Orient Express of the Wagons Lits company. |
| TRAMWAYS

Bimingham Central, Bowes Scott & Western (Incline Car), | Dudley & Stourbridge, City of Birmingham, Edinburgh & District, Electric Construction Co (sub-contract) | Glasgow Corporation, Indian Tramways, Perth (Scotland), South Staffordshire, Victor Harbour (Australia), | Walton-on-the-Naze Pier,

Blackpool 'Big Wheel' fairground cars to the order of W.K. Bassett. | |

Four Brown Marshalls carriages built in 1888 survive in Argentina. One of them, standard gauge No.760, known locally as an Overton type with a short body, end platforms and a clerestory roof, was the presidential coach used by Juan Peron and his wife Eva, the famous 'Evita'. This carriage still retains its original bedrooms, bathroom, kitchen and living room with wood burning stove and chimney! (Thanks to Sr Hector Cassano of the Museo Regional de Transportes, Cordoba, Argentina for this information).

On the narrow gauge Festiniog Railway in Wales, restoration has recently begun on two Brown Marshalls bogie carriages dating from 1872.

Some excellent pictures of Brown, Marshalls & Co vehicles have survived, all dating from 1887 and are reproduced in the rest of this chapter. Two for the Taff Vale Railway are shown here – a 3 plank mineral wagon and a meat van.

John Watkins

John Watkins

4 wheel, 2nd class coach for the London, Tilbury and Southend Railway No.35.

John Watkins

Brake-third coach for the London, Tilbury and Southend Railway No.20.

8 ton Brake Van No.7 Hull, Barnsley & West Riding Junction Railway & Dock Company, renamed the Hull & Barnsley Railway after 30th June 1905.
John Watkins

John Watkins

6 wheel Coach No.55 for Great North of Scotland Railway.

THE METROPOLITAN
Amalgamated Railway Carriage & Wagon Co., Ltd.
Incorporating

THE PATENT SHAFT & AXLETREE CO., Ltd., and DOCKER BROS., Ltd.

Constructors of RAILWAY CARRIAGES, WAGONS, TRAMCARS of all types.
Railway Carriage and Wagon Ironwork of every description.

Iron and Steel Underframes.   Railway Wheels and Axles.   Weldless Steel Tyres.

Iron and Steel Axles.   Bridges.   Roofs.   Turntables.   Tanks.

Switches and Crossings.   Open Hearth Steel Plates.   Bars, Sheets, Angles, Channels and Girders.

"BRUNSWICK" WELDLESS DISC WHEEL.
PRESSED STEEL BOGIE TRUCKS.

DOCKER BROS.' High Class Varnishes, Paints & Fine Colors for all Climates.
DOCKER'S "Hermator" Paints for Structural and every description of Engineering Work.

Head Offices: SALTLEY, BIRMINGHAM.   Telephone 6410 (Six Lines).

Telegrams: "Metro, Birmingham."

London Offices: 36, VICTORIA ST., WESTMINSTER, S.W.

Telephone 752 Westminster.   Telegrams: "Railcar, London."

CHAPTER 4

Metropolitan Amalgamated Railway Carriage and Wagon Company Ltd 1903-1918

From its beginning in 1902, Metropolitan Amalgamated was managed from the Oldbury offices in Broadwell Road, but soon transferred on 14 April 1904 to 1 Metropolitan Road, Saltley into a new office block whose reception halls and public rooms were adorned with transfers on panels bearing the arms of railways whose rolling stock had been supplied by the amalgamated companies. These transfers were made in Birmingham by Tearne & Sons and eventually totalled 150. Metropolitan Amalgamated paid a steady ten per cent dividend throughout the Edwardian years and built up substantial reserves to see the group through any further lean periods. This was done partly to provide against slack trade, but it also proved handy in cases such as the Mexican contract, paid for in what proved to be worthless Mexican bonds, leaving Metropolitan with a large unpaid bill. All renewals and extensions of buildings and plant were charged to revenue, no further capital being needed.

By agreement with the Dick, Kerr group, in 1903 Metropolitan gave up building trams, and instead took up three new lines – steam rail-motors, electric underground railway cars and Pullman cars. The Edwardian years were the heyday of the steam rail-motor, and three locomotive builders (Avonside, Kerr Stuart and Kitson) all employed Metropolitan Amalgamated to construct the bodywork for their rail-motors. Most of these were built for export, since the British railway companies had their own carriage works (the last one, the Great Central's carriage works at Dukinfield, being opened in 1910). Most of the rail-motors proved to be underpowered and were later replaced by (or divided into) separate locomotive and trailers. A splendid example built at Metropolitan's Britannia Works in 1905 has been returned to working order for private-hire use on the Pichi-Richi tourist railway in South Australia, where it is known as *The Coffee-Pot*.

Construction of rapid-transit trains by Metropolitan Amalgamated started in 1903 with 24 motor cars for the Central London Railway; these were the first multiple unit cars in Europe. They were followed between 1904-7 by 70 cars for the Metropolitan Railway's Uxbridge and Inner Circle services, 120 virtually fireproof cars for London's Hammersmith & City Line, ten electric locomotives for the District Line and 20 for the Metropolitan. The American-financed London Electric Railway group preferred to rely on imports (from America, France and Hungary) as a response to alleged over-pricing, to which Metropolitan reacted by taking a stake in La Construction SA of Manage in Belgium as a source of low-cost components. This may well have been a factor in the closure of the Lancaster and Britannia works in 1908.

A major source of information for the following account is a series of five articles by John Wright, published in The Times newspaper between 29 May and 7 June 1907. 'The group has recently received two orders each for 1,800 wagons, one for India, the other for Japan. The wagons for Japan were an urgent order required in Manchuria during the Russo-Japanese War; the first was completed in seven days and the entire order in four months, all six Metropolitan factories being involved'. The title of Wright's article was *'Post-Chaise to Wagons Lits'*, which proved prophetic when the group secured orders from the Wagons Lits company in the 1920s. The first order for British-type Pullman cars was for seven twelve-wheeled cars to form the London to Brighton 'Southern Belle' in 1908. Other luxury vehicles included a saloon in 1910 for the president of the Argentine Republic, reportedly as a gift. All these were timber-built on steel underframes, using Burma teak, oak, ash, mahogany, walnut, sycamore, deal and pitchpine.

In 1912 the company's name was changed to Metropolitan Carriage Wagon & Finance Co Ltd, Docker explaining to shareholders that there was as much money to be made from hire-purchase finance as from manufacture. At that time however, money was the cause of much labour unrest in the country, shop floor workers seeking higher wages and trade union recognition. Eventually strikes broke out, many in the Midlands, and whilst some grievances were quickly settled, one at the neighbouring Birmingham Railway Carriage & Wagon Works, Smethwick, in April 1913, had a serious effect on the Metropolitan company. All of its workers from the Saltley, Oldbury and Wednesbury factories eventually came out in sympathy with their BRCW counterparts and all production stopped. The strike caused great hardship for the workers and a distress fund was started, whilst many local butchers, bakers and greengrocers donated food. A hunger march was staged from Birmingham to Liverpool and back which took 16 days to cover the 280 mile round trip. This not only gained public support but highlighted the dispute nationally and after 11 weeks a settlement was reached, to the satisfaction of the unions, management and workforce.

In August 1914 the First World War broke out, which at first wasn't taken too seriously, the confident opinion in the country was that 'it would all be over by Christmas'. This was not to be and very soon the Metropolitan groups' factories were engaged on government contracts including building some of the world's first tanks.

The idea of the first successful tank was conceived in September 1915 by a Major W G Wilson whilst working on a project for a military trench-crossing machine at William Foster & Company, the well known steam traction engine manufacturer from Lincoln. Together with a director of Fosters, William Tritton (later Sir William Tritton), they designed, and had built, a vehicle in the extremely short time of ten weeks, straight off the drawing board!

On the morning of 26 January 1916, military history was made as the first workable example of what was later to be called 'the tank' was driven from the works of William Foster along the road to the station for final despatch to Hatfield, Hertfordshire. At Hatfield, on Lord Salisbury's private golf

Above: From 1903 Metropolitan Amalgamated constructed body work for the rail-motors which had evolved at that time. Featured here is South Eastern & Chatham Railway Railmotor No.1 of 1905, with Metropolitan coachwork and Kitson 4 wheel tank engine.   *Historical Model Railway Society*

Below: 12 wheel Pullman Parlour car 'Bessborough' one of seven 12 wheeled Pullmans built for the London Brighton & South Coast Railway 'Southern Belle' in 1908, by Metropolitan Amalgamated at its Lancaster works. These Pullmans had the distinction of being the first British built and among the last rolling stock constructed at Lancaster before it closed in 1908.   *Historical Model Railway Society*

Below: On May 14th 1906 Prince Tsai Tse, cousin of the Emperor of China, paid a visit to the City of Birmingham where he was given lunch and feted by civic dignitaries. Later in the day he was conducted over the Saltley Works of Metropolitan Amalgamated Railway Carriage & Wagon Company where he watched the building of 30 carriages for the Shanghai-Nanking Railway.   *Author's collection*

Above: 10 Bo-Bo electric locomotives were built in 1906/7 for the Metropolitan Railway with 'Luggage van' style bodies and B.T.H. motors, eventually replaced by 300hp types. Note the coat of arms and the styles of the destination boards, later dispensed with.

Historical Model Railway Society

Below: Liverpool Overhead Railway 3rd class coach No.48 built by Metropolitan Amalgamated.

Kidderminster Railway Museum

Sleeping car built by Metropolitan Amalgamated Railway Carriage & Wagon Co., Saltley, in 1910 for the Leopoldina Railway, Brazil.

Author's collection

SELF-PROPELLED TRAIN FOR THE KHEDIVE OF EGYPT.

A HANDSOME motor train has been built for H.H. The Khedive of Egypt by the Metropolitan Railway Carriage & Finance Co., of Birmingham.

There are two carriages, a saloon car (which we illustrate), and a composite car. They are propelled by a benzol-electric system designed by the Allgemeine Elektricitats-Gesellschaft, of Berlin. The cars are arranged to be driven coupled together, each vehicle having a four-wheel motor bogie, the power to which is supplied by a 350 volt d.c. dynamo and a 100 volt exciter, coupled direct to a 100 h.p. benzol engine.

The power units on the two cars are arranged so that they can be operated as one complete

The length over body is 45-ft. 5-in., and over buffers 63-ft.; width over mouldings, 9-ft. 3-in.; height from rails to roof, 14-ft. 8-in., and height inside body, 9-ft. 5-in. The saloon is panelled in figured mahogany, the doors having cloisonné panels with the coat of arms in the centre. White Tynecastle decoration is used for the ceiling. Hit and miss ventilators, and deck lights to open in opposite directions are provided. Handsome electroliers and pendant fittings are fitted, all fittings being in satin-finished brass.

The saloon is furnished with one long table, a writing desk, side board, and two lounge settees, and several chairs upholstered in green buffalo hide. The floor is covered with a plain green Wilton pile carpet. The small private

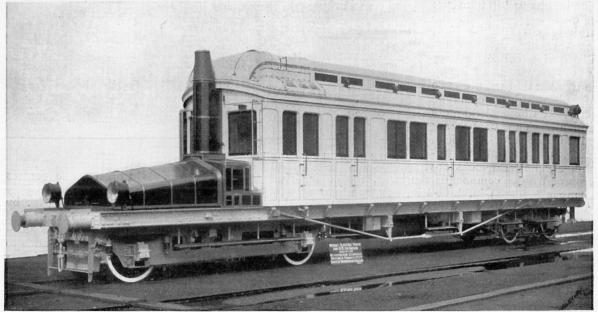

BENZOL ELECTRIC MOTOR COACH FOR THE KHEDIVE OF EGYPT.

unit by controlling from one or other of the driver's compartments.

Vibration is entirely eliminated, each power unit being isolated from the carriage, as it is mounted on an independent frame, well sprung, and supported inside the engine bogie frame.

Compressed air is used for starting the engines, a storage reservoir being provided. The carriages are equipped with the Westinghouse brake.

The carriage we illustrate is arranged with one large saloon 22-ft. long, having a sliding door at one end leading to an observation platform, and a swing door at the other end leading to a small compartment 7-ft. 6-in. long, beyond which through another swing door a short corridor, with a w.c. compartment on the left

hand and a lavatory compartment on the right hand side, leads to the driver's compartment. compartment is decorated in the same style and furnished with a bureau and bookcase, a small folding table, an arm chair and a settee. The lavatory and w.c. are finished in white enamel, with nickel plated fittings.

The composite carriage has two 2nd class compartments, three 3rd class, one luggage compartment, lavatory and w.c. compartments, with a short side corridor leading to the driver's compartment.

To obtain the best possible results in finishing off the exterior of the coaches they are faced with Lysaght's charcoal-finish steel panel plates, which are painted ivory white, lined with gold.

This rather exotic – and luxurious – vehicle is a far cry from the saloon coach built in 1845 for the Khedive, which is shown in the Metro-Cammell advertisement on page 4.

Above: Mark 2 Tank (No.577) under construction, winter 1916/17. Initially used as unarmoured training vehicles, some eventually ended up going into action.
Tank Museum Collection

Below: Mark V 'female' Tank being loaded onto a 'Rectank' wagon in 1918. 'Female' tanks were fitted with one Hotchkiss and four Vickers Machine guns, 'males' had four Hotchkiss machine guns and two six-pounders. Interestingly, during the First World War experimental caterpillar tractors were known as landships, and were within the domain of the Admiralty, hence the Naval Officer in the photograph.
Tank Museum Collection

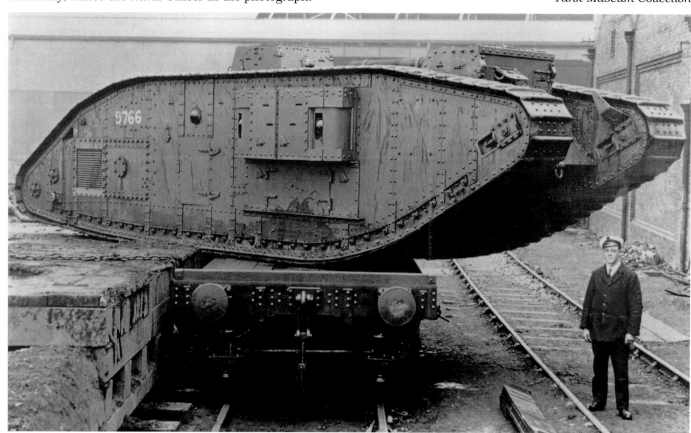

course, a series of front line obstacles had been laid, through which a series of trials were carried out with the machine, at the beginning of February 1916, in front of eminent military officers, cabinet ministers and even King George V. The military was so impressed with the way the tank made light work of the obstacles, that the War Office immediately ordered a hundred machines, twenty-five from Fosters and seventy-five from Metropolitan Carriage Wagon & Finance Company.

The first fifty tanks built were sent to France at the end of August 1916, for use in the Battle of the Somme offensive early in September. However, through a series of mishaps and breakdowns, only about half of them were fit for use on the morning they first went into action, 15 September 1916, at the Battle of Flers.

Initially, Metropolitan Carriage's Patent Shaft works at Old Park, Wednesbury produced some of these tanks but as the war progressed with a demand for more tanks, they and Fosters were joined by other companies, building bigger and better models.

Metropolitan's Oldbury works also become involved as evidenced by the survival, on adjacent waste land, of a concrete ramp used for tank testing, and later 'appropriated' by local children as a bicycle switch-back ride.

Known Customers of Metropolitan Carriage 1903-1918

Steam Rail-Motors (jointly with locomotive builders)

Belfast & County Down (1905/6 Kitson)	Central Rio Grande (1914)	Madras Railway (1905 Avonside)	South Eastern & Chatham (1905 Kitson)
Buenos Aires Midland (1909 Avonside)	Central South African (1906 Kitson)	Mauritius (1907 Kerr Stuart)	South Manchunan (1910 Kitson?)
Cape Government (1905 North British)	Egyptian State (1910 Hunslet)	Northern Nigerian (1908?)	United Rlwys of Havana (1905 Beyer Peacock)
	Italian State (1907 Kerr Stuart)	Rhymney (1907 Hudswell Clarke)	Western Tramways (1910 Kitson)
	Japanese Govt (1906 Yorkshire?)	South Australian (1905 Kitson)	
	La Guaira & Caracas (1907)		

Other Railway Orders

Antofagasta,
Argentine North Eastern,
Argentine Presidential Saloon (1910),
Argentine Transandine,
Arica-La Paz,
Barsi (India),
Barranqilla,
Belfast & County Down,
Bengal-Nagpur,
Brazil Great Southern,
Buenos Aires Great Southern,
Buenos Aires Midland,
Buenos Aires Western,
ER Calthrop (saloon),
Cape Central, Cape Government,
Central Argentine,
Central Northern Argentine,
Central Chubut (Argentine),
Central of Peru,
Central South African,
Central Uruguay,
Chilian Longitudina,
Cordoba & Rosario,
Cyprus Government,
Dalgety & Co, (contractor),
County Donegal,
Egyptian Delta Light Railways,
Egyptian State,
Federated Malay States,
Glasgow & South Western,
Gold Coast,
Great Central,
Great Indian Peninsular,
Great Southern & Western,
Great Western (Hammersmith & City),
Isle of Man,
Jamaica,
Jersey Eastern,
Kena-Aswan,
Kiangsu-Chekiang,
Leopoldina,
Liverpool Overhead,
LB & SCR (South London and
Crystal Palace a c. services),
LNWR,
Lourenco Marques,
Luxor-Aswan,
Malacca,
Manila,
Matheson (agent),
Metropolitan,
Metropolitan District,
Mexican National,
Midland of Uruguay,
Midland of Western Australia,
Natal Government,
New Zealand,
North British,
North Staffordshire,
North Western of Peru,
Paraguay Central,
Paulista,
Mr F Pound (Travelling Church 1908),
Pullman Car Company (1908 Brighton Train),
Railway & Works Co, Rhodesia,
San Salvador,
Sao Paulo,
Shanghai-Nanking,
Royal Siamese,
Sierra Leone,
South Africa,
South Indian,
South Eastern & Chatham (1903 Royal Saloon),
South Manchurian,
Southern Nigerian,
Sudan Government,
Table Bay Harbour,
Taff Vale,
Taltal (Chile),
Tientsin-Pukow,
Tralee and Dingle,
West Clare,
Western Oasis (Egypt),
War Office.

Pullman Cars

The 1908 Southern Belle (London to Brighton) was composed of seven twelve-wheeled Pullman cars named:

Alberta, Belgravia, Bessborough, Cleopatra, Grosvenor, Princess Helen and Verona.

Petrol Railcars and Inspection Cars

Assam-Bengal; Benguela; Egypt; New Zealand; Nigeria; Rhodesia.

Above: One of the twenty Metrovick locomotives at work on the Metropolitan Railway in the 1920s. Introduced in 1922, to work fast trains to Rickmansworth and Watford, the class had four 300hp motors giving a top speed of 65mph. Two locos, No.12 *Sarah Siddons* and No.5 *John Hampden* still survive long after the others went for scrap in the 1960s and 70s. *C. J. Walker collection*

Left: The Bo-Bo locos were featured in this advert for trains to the very first FA Cup Final at Wembley.

Below: An advertisement from the 1921 *Railway Year Book*.

The METROPOLITAN
CARRIAGE, WAGON & FINANCE COMPANY, Ltd.,

Incorporating
{ THE PATENT SHAFT & AXLETREE CO., LTD.
DOCKER BROTHERS, LTD.
THE WILLINGSWORTH IRON CO., LTD.
TAYLOR BROS. & CO., LTD.

AUTHORISED CAPITAL - - £10,675,000.

Manufacturers of
RAILWAY CARRIAGES,   WAGONS,
STEEL UNDERFRAMES,
RAILWAY WHEELS & AXLES OF ALL TYPES,
BRIDGES,   ROOFS,   TURNTABLES,
TANKS,   SWITCHES & CROSSINGS.

Specialities : ELECTRIC ROLLING STOCK & EQUIPMENT.

CHAPTER 5

Metropolitan Carriage Wagon and Finance Company Ltd 1919-1928

During the 1914-18 War, Metropolitan Carriage in collaboration with Vickers Ltd, the engineering and armament manufacturers, used part of its cash reserves in 1917 to buy control of the Westinghouse electrical works at Trafford Park, Manchester whose American owners decided to sell. Metropolitan's Chairman Dudley Docker had already seen a good future for railway electrification with the company's involvement in electric trains in and around London, and also advantages in close co-operation between electrical and rolling-stock suppliers, both at home and abroad. This view was shared by Vickers Limited, and for their part it gave them a foothold in the rolling stock business in which they already had interests. This foothold was further strengthened in 1919 when Vickers took over Metropolitan on acquiring its shares, and one immediate result was the formation in 1919 of a subsidiary company, the Metropolitan-Vickers Electrical Co Ltd ('Metrovick' for short), which was able to put together 'package deals' in railway electrification. The fact that Dudley Docker had become a director of the Metropolitan Railway and the LB&SCR (and later Southern Railway) must have had a great influence on this decision.

The backlog of demand caused by the 1914-18 War kept the various factories busy for several years, and the first two postwar rapid-transit orders were tube trains for the Bakerloo line's Watford extension, and one hundred oval-end-window steel cars for London's District line, helped by a Government grant to ease the transition from wartime to peacetime construction. These cars were referred to initially as Tanks, partly from their appearance and partly because the Old Park works where they were built had made tanks during the War. As with the tanks, they were jig-built, every similar piece in any car being interchangeable, with no 'cut and fit' workmanship. They were very strong vehicles, and gave 42 years service. In 1923-5 Metropolitan built its first air-door London tube trains (more followed in 1926/7 and 1930-4), some of which ran until 1990 on the Isle of Wight. Main-line suburban electric trains (mostly with Metrovick equipment) were built around this period for the LNWR, LMSR, the Metropolitan Railway, the Southern Railway, the Central Argentine Railway and for suburban services in Bombay. Saltley works also built 21 electric locomotives (disguised as 'milk vans' for the Southern Railway's Croydon and Sutton a.c. services. At the 1924 Wembley Exhibition, the main attraction on Metropolitan's stand was a saloon for King Fuad of Egypt, with a high arched roof that concealed a double ceiling designed to deflect or absorb the heat of the sun, a standard Metropolitan design feature for hot countries.

The use of Pullman cars on British railways increased considerably during the 1920s, and after about 50 wooden Pullmans had been built by other Midlands firms, Metropolitan secured orders in 1926/7 for 30 steel Pullman cars to work on the LNER, starting with the *Queen of Scots*. The Pullman Car Company's practice was to christen its first class cars with girls'

names, but so many were now needed that they had to use some rather mythological examples such as *Belinda, Cassandra, Eunice, Evadne, Lucille, Marcelle, Octavia, Philomel, Rainbow, Therma, Theodora, Ursula* and various Greek goddesses. Three of these cars, *Zena, Lucille* and *Ione*, have been nicely restored in recent years to form part of the Venice Simplon-Orient Express British Pullman train.

Metropolitan's prestige as an employer stood at a high level, as did that of its apprenticeship scheme. The Works Committee System introduced at Saltley proved a great success, and from 1917 it was possible for Metropolitan employees to become shareholders. Dudley Docker helped to set up the Midland Employers Federation, the British Electrical & Allied Manufacturers Association, and the Federation of British Industries. He also helped to start Wagon Repairs Limited, founded in 1918, which brought to an end the need for each owner of private hire wagons to maintain its own chain of repair works. The Association of Railway Carriage & Wagon Manufacturers, to which all the firms belonged, campaigned successfully against a plan by Sir Eric Geddes to build steel rolling-stock at the government-owned Woolwich Arsenal.

In 1928, the link between Metropolitan-Vickers and Metropolitan CW&F was broken, in a controversial deal in which Metrovick was sold to its American rival, the General Electric Company, parent of British Thomson-Houston. GE placed both firms under the control of a holding company, Associated Electrical Industries Ltd, but allowed them to compete for power supply contracts while rationalising the manufacture of traction equipment. Not until January 1959 did AEI trade under its own name, and even this was short-lived.

Wagons Lits

Of all the British rolling-stock firms, Metropolitan's was the name best known on the Continent of Europe. The Company in 1926-29 built cars for some of Europe's most prestigious trains, run by the *Compagnie Internationale des Wagons Lits et des Grands Express Européens*. The Wagons Lits company bought 384 steel vehicles from British builders between 1922 and 1929, the shares being Metropolitan 149, Leeds Forge 70 and BRCW 165.

Until 1914, Wagons Lits generally ordered its cars from builders in the countries where they were to work, the only British order being three Brown, Marshalls dining cars for the Calais-Brindisi P&O boat train in 1892. Reasons for the 1920s bulk orders were the British firms' quick recovery from the War, their experience in steel construction, the availability of British capital through the newly-formed international Sleeping Car Share Trust and the British builders' willingness to offer 'easy terms'. Metropolitan's own ledgers have not been studied, but those of BRCW in the Staffordshire Record Office show that in 1926-29 Wagons Lits was spreading the payment for its new cars over 25 years. With a six-year wartime gap, the final instalment wasn't paid until 1951.

1927 trailer car built at Saltley for the London Electric Railway, which came into existence in 1910 after the amalgamation of various lines.   *Author's collection*

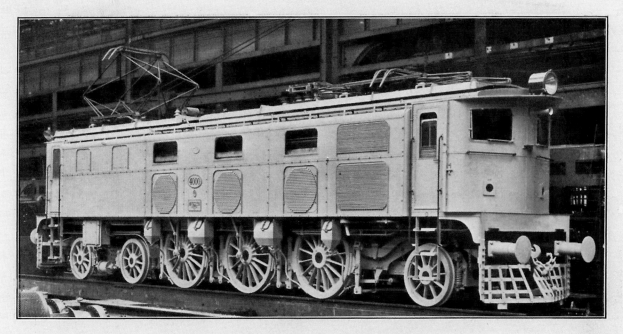

Metrovick 2,160-H.P. High-Speed Passenger Locomotive.

The electrical equipment includes six motors each developing 360 H.P. and having Metrovick electro-pneumatic control gear.
The two-wheel pony works in conjunction with the adjacent driving axle so as to form virtually a four-wheel truck.

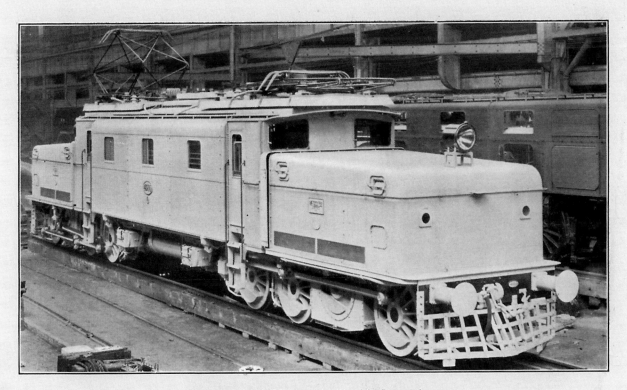

Metrovick 2,600-H.P. Articulated Freight Locomotive.

The total weight of 120 tons is available for adhesion. The body is carried on two trucks coupled by a flexible joint.
Regenerative braking is provided, and the locomotive operates on a 1,500-volt supply from overhead lines.

ELECTRIC LOCOMOTIVES FOR THE GREAT INDIAN PENINSULA RAILWAY.

Egyptian railways had been good customers since Joseph Wright's days and the mid 1920s saw more orders, including this fine 1st class carriage. A saloon coach for H.M. The King of Egypt was displayed at the British Empire Exhibition in 1924.
Author's collection

Indian Railways was, and is, a huge undertaking and, at various times, attempts were made to introduce some standardisation to locos and rolling stock. This 1926 built broad gauge brake van is but a modest example of the Indian Railway standards.

Author's collection

35

Railway Customers of Metropolitan Carriage Wagon and Finance Co Ltd 1919-1928

Antofagasta Chili & Bolivia (1926)	Egyptian State (1927)	LMSR (1925-7)	South Africa (various)
Benguela (1925)	Federated Malay States (1926)	LNER (1921)	South Eastern & Chatham (1922)
Buenos Aires Great Southern (1924/5)	Glasgow & South Western (1920)	Madras & Southern Mahratta (1924-6)	South Indian (1923/5)
Burma (1924/5)	Great Western of Brazil (1921)	Manila Rly (1925)	Southern (1923/8)
Caledonian (1921)	India (North Western) (1925)	Metropolitan (1920/6)	Sudan Government (1923)
Central Argentine (1928)	Isle of Man (1923/5)	Nizam of Hyderabad (1928)	Trans-Zambesi (1921/2)
Central of Brazil (1922-8)	Jodhpur-Bikaner (1924-8)	North Staffordshire (1922)	Uganda (1925)
Central Uruguay (1927/8)	Katanga (1924/5)	Palestine (1921/2)	Underground Group (1920-7)
Earl of Derby (horsebox 1923)	Kenya & Uganda (1926/8)	Pullman Car Company (1926/8)	Union Miniere (Congo) (1925)
Ebbw Vale (1919, 1929)	Kowloon-Canton (1925)	Royal Siamese State (1920)	War Office (various)
Egypt (royal saloon 1924)	Lancashire & Yorkshire (1921)	Sierra Leone (1924/7)	Wagons Lits Co (1926-8)
	Leopoldina (1926-8)		

Drawings were also prepared for vehicles to be built by Construccion Naval of Bilbao, Spain.
Drawings were prepared in 1925 for Moscow suburban trains, to be built in Russia.

The move from timber-built to steel-built rolling stock began with a need for termite-resistant vehicles for tropical countries, followed by the fireproof-vehicles required by the London tube railways. In main-line railway work the change was prompted by considerations of speed and safety, some railways (including the French) permitting higher speeds for all-steel trains. Another factor favouring a shift to British builders was the availability of the wartime train ferry ships, one of which was used in 1922 to move 40 Leeds Forge sleeping cars from Immingham to Calais; from 1924, there was a regular service from Harwich to Zeebrugge. Continental rolling-stock was built to a slightly larger loading gauge than British, so the cars were run to the ports minus steps and handrails, mounted on screw-action travelling-jacks which permitted some transverse movement to avoid lineside obstacles. However, 20 Metropolitan sleeping cars for Spain's broad (1,674 mm) gauge railways were loaded by crane at Swansea docks in 1927 and shipped direct, as were some BRCW vehicles for Egypt.

Metropolitan's deliveries to Wagons Lits comprised 60 sleeping cars, 15 diners, 40 Pullmans and 34 baggage vans. Lord Dalziel, then chairman of both the Pullman Car Company and Wagons Lits, hoped to repeat on the Continent the success of his Pullman trains in Britain. Best-known was the London-Paris *Golden Arrow (Fléche d'Or)*, for which Metropolitan built 15 Pullmans, with 32 individual armchair seats in two saloons and two coupés. They had identical carpeting and upholstery to the British Pullman cars which formed the train between London and Dover, and some passengers thought they were going to travel throughout in the same Pullman train - until they arrived at Dover (or Calais) and had to change to the Pullman lounge on the s.s. *Canterbury*. One of the Metropolitan Pullmans (4018) occupies a place of honour in the French Railway's museum at Mulhouse, displayed in the brown and cream livery used when these cars were new. Many of the other Pullmans built in 1926-28 were later converted to diners.

The Metropolitan sleeping cars were of two main types, S and LX. Both had the full range of Wagons Lits gadgets, such as water-carafe, glassholders, mirrors, non-rattle coat hangers, blue light, main light, reading light, and a holder for a fob watch. Fixtures included chain and lock for the compartment door, alarm handle, call bell button for conductor, moveable ventilation-slots in the door, adjustable window louvres to deflect smoke, a wall cupboard, and a radiator under the window. The 30 LX-type sleepers, built for the Calais-Riviera *Train Bleu*, had the largest sleeping compartments in Europe. Each compartment had a separate washroom, closed off by curved floor-to-ceiling double doors with a sharkskin scuffing strip at the base. The decoration was by Maple & Co Ltd of London and Taylor-Lord & Morrison of Edinburgh, and the marquetry was by A Done & Co of Chelmsford, who still exist. The S-type cars in Spain ran from 1927 to 1961, and the LX cars formed the *Blue Train* from 1929 to 1969. Four of them run today in the *Venice Simplon-Orient Express*, and four others plus two vans are in the *Nostalgie Orient Express*.

The 34 *fourgons* were designed to take passengers' heavy luggage, mails, and the company's own courier parcel service which was operated in the *Trains de Luxe*. Separate compartments inside could be sealed by Customs on departure, and thus permit transit through intermediate countries without inspection. In the days before air freight, this was an important (and profitable) part of the company's business. Vital spare parts for machines supplied to the Middle East could arrive in Istanbul quickly by the *Simplon-Orient-Express*, and be transferred there to the *Taurus Express* for Syria or Iraq. Twenty of the *fourgons* were also fitted with a shower compartment for the Istanbul and Paris-Rome services. One of the Wagons Lits legends relates to a lady who, in 1934, was about to take a shower when she realised that the van was being uncoupled, due to a hot axlebox. She narrowly missed being separated from all her belongings and most of her apparel!

Metropolitan Carriage Wagons Lits Co Orders 1926-1929. TOTAL 149

Stock numbers	Type of vehicle built	Year	Total	Original Allocation
1263-1296	Baggage Van	1927-9	34	*Trains de Luxe*
2933-2942	Sleeping car (S1)	1926	10	*Trains de Luxe*
3361-3380	Sleeping car (S4)	1927	20	*Spain (Norte)*
3391-3405	Restaurant car	1929	15	*Trains de Luxe and Turkey*
3466-3495	Sleeping car (LX)	1929	30	*Blue Train*
4016-4030	Pullman car	1926	15	*Golden Arrow*
4086-4090	Pullman car	1927	5	*Golden Arrow*
4111-4130	Pullman car	1927	20	*North Star*

Above: Third class Pullman Parlour car No.74, one of the thirty all-steel Pullmans built in 1928 initially for use on the L.N.E.R. including the 'Queen of Scots' service. No.74 is seen here in post 1930 livery, the word Pullman appearing in a narrow umber band, which prior to 1930 was against a white background. Only first class and composite cars were given names by the Pullman Company.

Author's collection

Below: Interior view of third class car No.74. Note the ornate cover of the roof ventilator and lamps on every table.

Author's collection

NEW BRAKE VANS FOR THE INTERNATIONAL SLEEPING CAR COMPANY.

These Vehicles are being Built by the Metropolitan Carriage, Wagon & Finance Co. Ltd. for International Sleeping Car Services.

The bogie brake vans illustrated herewith (34 in number) are at present being constructed at the works of the Metropolitan Carriage, Wagon & Finance Co. Ltd., at Saltley, Birmingham, to the order of the International Sleeping Car Company for use in conjunction with their various international services. The vans, with the upper panels light coloured, are intended for use on any of the Continental Pullman services, and the other cars for any international *de luxe* type trains, the finish being in accord with that of the well-known "Blue Trains." Those to be equipped with bathrooms are intended for running on the Orient and other long-distance expresses.

by 10-lb. joist sections, with intermediate crossbars of 5-in. by $2\frac{1}{2}$-in. by 10·22-lb. channel. The portion of the underframe between the two main joist section crossbars is built up of channel crossbars and longitudinals of the same section as the solebars in order to give sufficient strength to carry the brake gear, accumulators, &c. The whole frame is braced by 3-in. by $\frac{1}{4}$-in. flats.

The body is an entirely steel structure of pressed pillars, angle-section cantrails, pressed-section waist rail stiffened with a heavy section mould, and pressed carlines and purlins. The side and end plating is of $\frac{1}{8}$-in. mild-steel plates throughout. The roof sheeting is of $\frac{1}{16}$-in. mild-steel plate, canvassed on the underside to provide

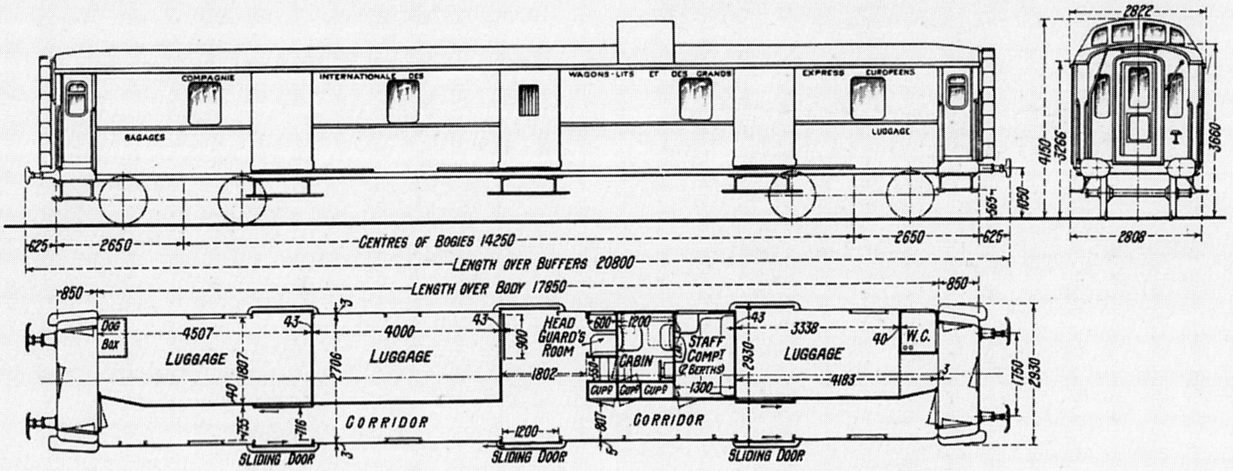

Elevations and Plan of Brake Van for International Sleeping Car Services.

The vehicles have the following leading dimensions and weights :—

Length, outside platforms	19 m. 550 (64 ft. $1\frac{5}{8}$ in.)
Length of body	17 m. 850 (58 ft. $6\frac{11}{16}$ in.)
Length over headstocks	19 m. 550 (64 ft. $1\frac{5}{8}$ in.)
Length over buffers	20 m. 800 (68 ft. $2\frac{7}{8}$ in.)
Width of underframe	2 m. 602 (8 ft. $6\frac{3}{8}$ in.)
Width of body over cornice joint plate	2 m. 712 (8 ft. $10\frac{11}{16}$ in.)
Width over end steps	2 m. 930 (9 ft. $7\frac{1}{4}$ in.)
Width over side steps	2 m. 930 (9 ft. $7\frac{1}{4}$ in.)
Width over sliding door top guides	2 m. 8,285 (9 ft. $3\frac{1}{4}$ in.)
Normal buffer height	1 m. 050 (3 ft. $5\frac{3}{8}$ in.)
Total height (rail to top of caboose roof sheeting)	4 m. 150 (13 ft. $7\frac{5}{16}$ in.)
Total height (rail to top of main roof sheeting)	3 m. 660 (12 ft. 0 in.)
Centres of bogies	14 m. 250 (46 ft. 9 in.)
Centres of buffers	1 m. 750 (5 ft. $8\frac{7}{8}$ in.)
Maximum weight of van, empty	38 metric tons (37·4 tons)
Maximum load	6 metric tons (5·9 tons)

The bogies are of the usual Commonwealth cast-steel type, this being the standard of the Wagons-Lits Company.

In view of the lighter weight and shorter length, the structure of the underframe departs from the design used for the same company's sleeping and dining cars. A similar but lightened form of cast-steel frame end is used, but the heavy longitudinal centre girder has been replaced by a somewhat lighter structure. The solebars are of 9-in. by 3-in. by 17·46-lb. channel sections, and the two main crossbars 9-in. by 4-in. by 21-lb. joist sections. From these crossbars to the end castings run longitudinals of 4-in. by 3-in.

some measure of insulation against sound and variation of temperature. Partitions are of 4-mm. steel plate, combined with pressings, and are connected directly to the underframe crossbars.

The floor is made up of heavy red deal matchboards assembled as units, and the inside partition work is of red deal matching in oak frames. The corridor partition above the cantrail is also made up of a series of pressings. The interior of the car is divided into four luggage compartments, with a compartment for the use of the personnel in the centre. Adjoining this is the compartment of the *Chef du Train,* and the steps leading to the look-out, which is provided with windows giving a view over the roof of the train. In one corner of the car is a lavatory for the use of the staff, whilst twenty of these cars will be fitted with an elaborate bathroom for the use of passengers, ample supplies of hot water being available.

Access to the luggage compartment is through wide sliding doors from the corridor and the outside of the car. The personnel compartment is provided with two berths for the use of the staff as well as a wash-basin and ample cupboard accommodation. In the look-out are the various steam, vacuum and Westinghouse gauges, as well as the emergency brake valves. The portion of the car occupied by the staff is heated by steam, while, in addition, electric radiators are provided on the cars destined for use on the Swiss Railways. Lighting throughout is by means of the Dick system. The exterior of the car is finished in cellulose with a certain number of gold lines, while the Wagons-Lits Company's monogram is placed on the lower panel of the door in the centre of the car.

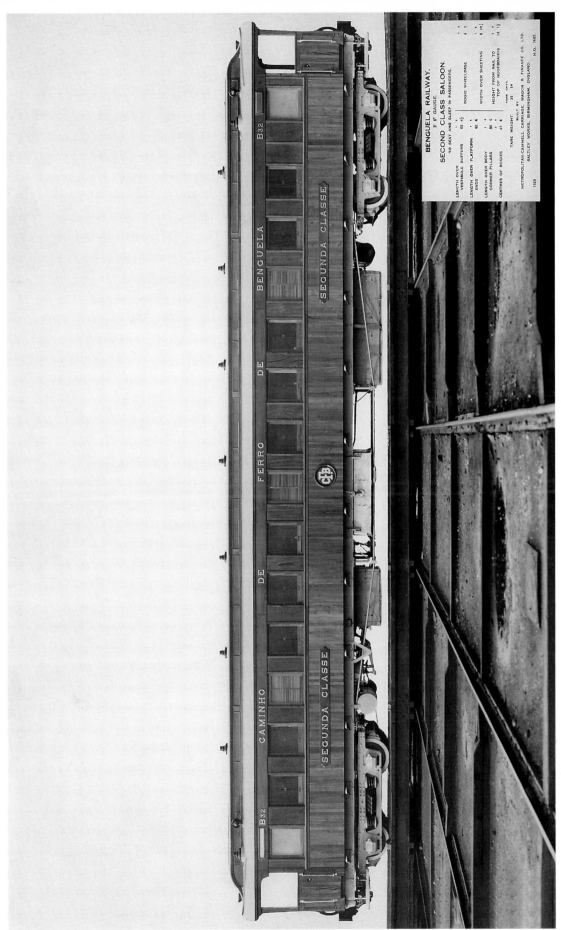

BENGUELA RAILWAY.
3' 6" GAUGE.
SECOND CLASS SALOON.
TO SEAT AND SLEEP 39 PASSENGERS.

LENGTH OVER VESTIBULE BUFFERS	65 4½	
LENGTH OVER PLATFORM ENDS	62 6	BOGIE WHEELBASE 5 1
LENGTH OVER BODY CORNER PILLARS	56 6	WIDTH OVER SHEETING 8 10
CENTRES OF BOGIES	47 6	HEIGHT FROM RAIL TO TOP OF ROOFBOARDS 12 1½

TARE WEIGHT: TONS CWTS. 35 14

BUILT BY
METROPOLITAN-CAMMELL CARRIAGE, WAGON & FINANCE CO. LTD.
SALTLEY WORKS, BIRMINGHAM, ENGLAND.
1929. H.O. 7685.

Second class seating and sleeping saloon for the 3' 6" Benguela Railway. Built by Metropolitan-Cammell Wagon & Finance Company, Saltley, in 1929. Seating and sleeping was provided for 39 passengers which must have been rather cramped! The overall contract comprised five separate types, all built on similar lines. In addition to the type illustrated here, there were first class saloons, 'native coaches', dining cars and a private saloon. All the vehicles were said to be 'of handsome exterior and noteworthy for the excellence of workmanship and finish, with the equipment being in all cases fully abreast of the most exacting requirements of modern railway travel.'

Author's collection

Above: Fifty of these 35-ton hopper ballast wagons were completed at Saltley in 1928 for the metre gauge Cordoba Central Railway in Argentina, Designed by Metropolitan, they were required to discharge their contents at the same rate as broad or standard gauge wagons.

Below: A new design 45-ton steel bogie covered wagon was also made in 1928 for the 5' 6" gauge Buenos Aires Great Southern Railway, Argentina.

Left: Detail of the Gresley 6-wheel bogie built by Leeds Forge and used on Central Argentine Railway stock introduced in 1928, said at the time to be 'the longest and heaviest vehicles ever built on the Gresley articulated system'.

CHAPTER 6

The Metropolitan-Cammell Carriage, Wagon & Finance Co Ltd (Metro-Cammell) 1929-1939

The early 1920s saw the formation of a new rolling-stock combine with the potential to rival the Metropolitan group. It was headed by steelmaker and shipbuilder Cammell, Laird & Co Ltd, whose munitions works at Kings Field Road, Nottingham was being converted to build all-steel rolling stock. Cammell Laird had gained control of Leeds Forge Co Ltd, the Newlay Wheel Co Ltd and the Midland Railway-Carriage & Wagon Co Ltd, and Leeds Forge had already acquired (and closed) the Bristol Wagon and Carriage Company Ltd. The companies were not merged, but undertook joint tendering, advertising and promotion.

The Midland Railway-Carriage & Wagon Co Ltd, which had remained independent when Metropolitan Amalgamated was formed in 1902, had been based at Shrewsbury, but in 1907 it bought from Lord Norton a 62-acre site at Leigh Road, Washwood Heath, on which to build a new works. The site had previously been used for an isolation hospital in surrounding farmland. The factory built in 1911 by H Arnold & Son Ltd of Doncaster, with structural steelwork from Dorman Long & Co Ltd, was laid out on spacious lines with traversers able to move any foreseeable size of railway vehicles. The new works opened in 1912, replacing Shrewsbury. The Midland Works at Washwood Heath is today the home of what we knew as Metro-Cammell, but the Midland Railway-Carriage & Wagon Co Ltd was only wound up in 1948, having been kept in being until then to run the Metropolitan group's wagon hire business and as landlord of Washwood Heath works.

Reverting to Cammell Laird, this company secured several London tube train orders between 1919 and 1925, and built large numbers of steel hopper (and other) wagons, but after 1926 the Nottingham works was under-employed apart from building Sentinel-Cammell steam railcars and some Bombay electric suburban trains. In a re-run of the 1902 merger, Dudley Docker persuaded Cammell Laird that the way forward was to merge their rolling stock activities with those of Metropolitan, the shares to be held 50% by Vickers and 50% by Cammell Laird.

The new joint title from January 1929 was Metropolitan-Cammell Carriage, Wagon and Finance Co Ltd. This kept alive the Cammell name, but not the Nottingham factory, which only traded under the new name for two years before closing in 1931 and eventually reverting to ordnance work. Some of the last vehicles built at Nottingham were subway cars for the Buenos Aires Terminal Central Railway in 1930. There was no attempt to conceal the need to eliminate over-capacity, and by 1931 Ashbury, Oldbury and Leeds Forge had also closed. This enabled the group to concentrate all its activities in the West Midlands (at Saltley, Washwood Heath and Wednesbury) where work in hand included the 1929 Wagons Lits orders, 28 steel suburban coaches for South Africa and electric trains for the metre gauge system in Madras and 150 wagons and 150 carriages for Rhodesia. Paint and varnish supplier Docker Brothers Limited had been excluded from the 1929 merger and regained its independence.

Above: A line of Pullman cars waiting delivery from the Midland Railway-Carriage & Wagon Company to the L.N.E.R. in 1923. Nearest the camera is 'Vera' a first class diner, followed by two more first class diners and a parlour car. These wooden-bodied Pullmans later gave way to all-steel. *Historical Model Railway Society*

Above: A 7 plank 12 ton mineral wagon belonging to the Midland Railway-Carriage Company hire fleet. The 'starred' plate at the front denotes its ownership.

Historical Model Railway Society

Below: Sierra Leone Development Company Ltd 30 ton steel bogie iron ore wagon with diamond frame bogies and 3' 6" gauge. It was built in 1931 by Metro-Cammell Carriage Wagon & Finance Company, Oldbury works.

B.J.R. Yates

SOUTH AFRICAN MINES

40-TON SIDE DISCHARGE HOPPER WAGON

FITTED WITH LINING PLATES & SKEFKO AXLEBOXES

3' 6" GAUGE

LENGTH OVER HEADSTOCKS	29' 9"	MAXIMUM WIDTH	8' 5¼"
CENTRES OF BOGIES	19' 3"	WHEELBASE OF BOGIES	5' 0"
HEIGHT FROM RAIL TO TOP	9' 6¾"	TARE	17 TONS 1 CWT. 2 QRS.

BUILT BY

METROPOLITAN-CAMMELL CARRIAGE, WAGON & FINANCE CO. LTD.,

SALTLEY WORKS. ENGLAND.

H.O. 6933 & 7060   1933   NEG. NO. 7780

A South African Mines 40 ton side discharge hopper wagon, built at Saltley in 1933 and fitted with 'Skefko' axleboxes.   *Author's collection*

Above: Following trials with a Sentinel-Cammell steam railcar in 1925, the L.M.S. took delivery of a further 12 in 1927 for use on branch lines. These cars took the L.M.S. stock numbers 4143-54 and seating was for 44 passengers. The photo shows one of the cars with coachwork by Cammell-Laird of Nottingham. The Sentinel power unit differed slightly from the trial car in that the coal bunker was filled through a trap door (visible on the roof) allowing the use of coaling chutes at locomotive sheds. There were also hinged panels on each side of the cab for filling the water tanks.

Author's collection

Below: One of 56 all steel motor cars built for the 4' 8½" gauge electric subway services of the Buenos Aires Terminal Central Railway in 1930. These were among the last vehicles constructed by Metropolitan-Cammell Carriage Wagon & Finance at its Nottingham works before it closed in 1931.

Author's collection

Two small experimental Bo-Bo diesel electric locos were built by Metropolitan and delivered to the Buenos Aires Great Southern Railway in 1929. CM201 had a 375hp eight-cylinder Beardmore diesel engine, while CM202 had a 420hp six-cylinder Sulzer engine. They were used on various duties to gain experience of diesel traction, but CM201 achieved a record longest non-stop run in South America, 1194km from Buenos Aires to Neuquen.

Another interesting order in the period was for the construction of six single-unit and two double articulated Sentinel-Cammell steam railcars for Roumanian State Railways. Cammell's Nottingham factory which had built steam railcars closed the previous year, so this order was fulfilled at the Midland Works.

The trade slump of the early 1930s brought about problems for Metro-Cammell especially for the shop floor workers, for at times the total productive labour strength was less than half. However, things could have been worse but for a decision by the company to apply its experience of steel railway carriages to the

Below: An article from *The Locomotive* magazine of October 1932.

SENTINEL-CAMMELL STEAM RAIL-CAR. ROUMANIAN STATE RYS.

Rail-cars for the Roumanian State Rys.

TO meet the competition of motor traffic, which is very keen in the districts served by some of the secondary lines, the Roumanian Railway Administration decided to work the traffic by rail-cars, and after considering many tenders and studying various systems, finally decided to purchase six single-unit and two double articulated Sentinel-Cammell steam rail-cars. We herewith reproduce a photograph of the first of the single unit rail-cars, which is now in service. The boiler compartment at the front of the car contains the oil-fired boiler, water tank, oil tank, controls, sand boxes, air brake compressor, etc., whilst the six cylinder 100/150-h.p. Sentinel engine, with cylinders 6 in. bore by 7 in. stroke, is slung from the underframe at the rear of the leading bogie, on to which it drives. The water-tube vertical boiler carries a working pressure of 300 lb. per sq in., while the steam is superheated to a temperature of from 650° to 750° Fahr. The drive is transmitted from the engine to a gearbox mounted on the driving axle by a cardan shaft. The all-steel body is mounted on a light underframe, on which the sides and roof are so arranged to form integral parts of a rigid structure.

The controls provided in the boiler compartment are duplicated in a driving compartment at the rear of the car. The Westinghouse air brake is fitted, as well as a screw hand brake, in each driver's compartment.

the second-class being covered in "Rexine" material. The third-class seats have cushions and backs of the lath and space type. Steps and handrails are provided at all doorways.

Electric light equipment on the "Dick" system provides for head and tail lamps, as well as for lighting the passenger compartments. Steam heating is provided and torpedo ventilators are fitted. The outside finish is in dark blue. These rail-cars were shipped by way of the Harwich-Zeebrugge train ferry, and were run on their own wheels overland to Roumania *via* Aachen, Passau, Hegyeshalon, Lokoshaza, and Curtici. The two double articulated cars will be completed this month and despatched by the same route.

The leading dimensions are :—Length over body, 58 ft. 6 in.; width overall, 9 ft. 6 in.; centres of bogies, 40 ft. 4 in.; wheelbase—driving bogie, 7 ft. 6 in.; carrying bogie, 6 ft. 6 in.; Wheels, diameter, 3 ft. 1⅝ in.

The power units with the control gear have been built at the Shrewsbury works of the Sentinel Waggon Works Ltd., and the cars by the Metropolitan-Cammell Carriage, Wagon, and Finance Co. Ltd. at their Midland Works, Birmingham.

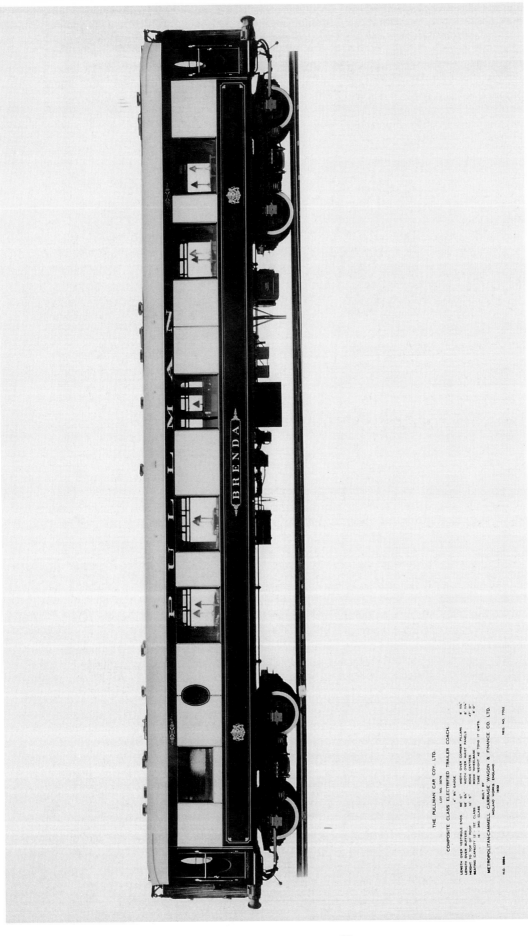

Pullman composite car 'Brenda' built in 1932 by Metropolitan-Cammell Carriage, Wagon & Finance Company at its Midland Works, Washwood Heath, for service on the all electric Pullman train 'Brighton Belle'. Seating capacity was 12 first class, 16 third class.

Author's collection

The all electric 'Brighton Belle'. Three five-car electric Pullman trains were built by Metro-Cammell in 1932 but usually two units were coupled together as pictured here. The third unit was kept as a standby.

T.P. Bye

47

construction of steel framed bus bodies and this is covered in Chapter 10.

The Metropolitan-Cammell Carriage, Wagon & Finance Co Ltd was reconstructed in 1934 as the Metropolitan-Cammell Carriage & Wagon Co Ltd, but with its capital (still owned in equal parts by Cammell Laird & Co Ltd and Vickers Ltd) reduced to match the slimmed-down production facilities. A welcome order in 1932 was for three five-car electric Pullman trains for the *Brighton Belle*, plus 23 single Pullmans for the other Southern Railway electric services to Brighton, Eastbourne and Worthing. The *Brighton Belle*, the world's first all electric Pullman train, ran until 1972, and its cars still exist, some of them in the VSOE Pullman train.

During 1934 orders included 700 low-sided vacuum-braked goods wagons of 12-ton capacity for the LMS for use with their container traffic while one hundred 30-ton open bogie wagons, utilising the Sheffield-Twinberrow patent bogie, were supplied for the San Paulo Railway in Brazil.

In 1935 an order for first and second class electric motor coaches was completed for the suburban areas around Johannesburg and Cape Town. 1936 saw the building of some experimental 6 car tube trains (some with streamlined cabs) for London Transport, followed by 79 three-car electric trains for the Rio de Janeiro suburban lines of the Central Railway of Brazil.

1933-36 saw a brief resumption of tramcar building. Edinburgh Corporation led the way in adopting mainly-metal lightweight bodies for trams, and bought fourteen from Metro-Cammell, who also built two prototype and fifty production cars for Johannesburg, and two body 'kits' for Leeds. No more tram orders were obtained until 1960, when Saltley Works built ten railers for Blackpool.

In 1938 the railway side was starting to recover with orders for over 700 London tube cars, 19 three-car trains for the Wirral lines of the LMS, and 64 articulated twin-sets for the North Tyneside lines of the LNER, both the latter shared with BRCW. Another contract was the 12 coach *Union Limited* for South Africa, which in 1946 became the *Blue Train*.

Other orders included goods wagons for home and overseas and road passenger vehicle bodies which ensured continued employment at the Birmingham area factories. However, war clouds were gathering over Europe and those uneasy days of peace were soon ended in 1939, as Britain, once again, went to war with Germany.

A Sheffield Twinberrow carriage bogie fitted with Framwel axleboxes. Built by Metro-Cammell Carriage & Wagon Company Ltd for use by the Ceylon Railway 5' 6" gauge.
B.J.R. Yates

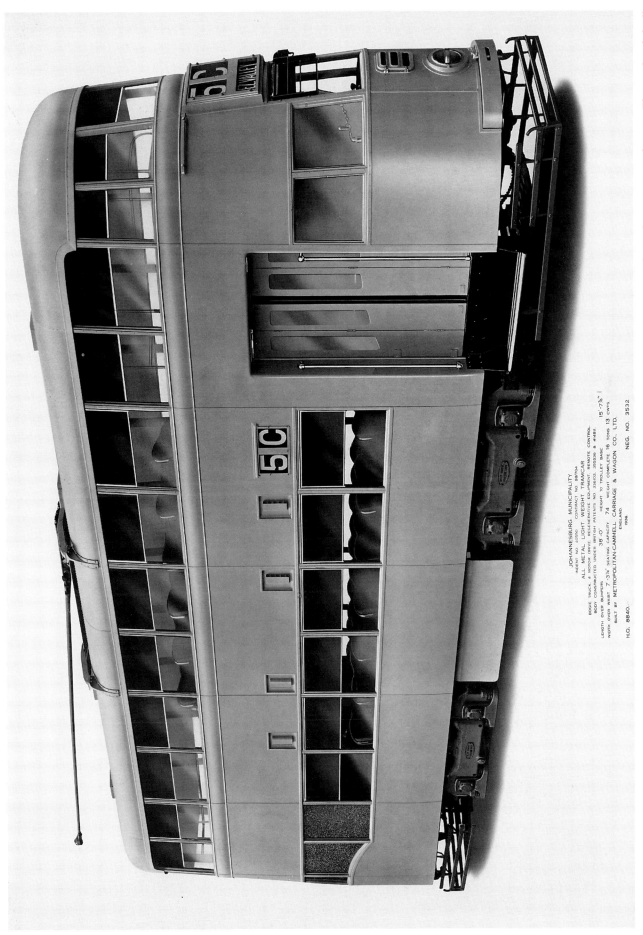

JOHANNESBURG MUNICIPALITY
INDENT NO. 40550   CONTRACT NO. 98704
ALL METAL LIGHT WEIGHT TRAMCAR
BOGIE TRUCK. 4 MOTOR DRIVE. REGENERATIVE EQUIPMENT. REMOTE CONTROL.
BODY CONSTRUCTED UNDER BRITISH PATENTS NO 336103, 335536 & 414811
LENGTH OVER BUMPERS   38' 0"   HEIGHT TO TROLLEY BASE   15'-7⅞"
WIDTH OVER WAIST   7-3¼"   SEATING CAPACITY   74   WEIGHT COMPLETE   16 TONS   13 CWTS.
BUILT BY METROPOLITAN-CAMMELL CARRIAGE & WAGON CO. LTD.
ENGLAND.
1936.

H.Q. 8840.   NEG. NO. 3532

After the 1930s world trade slump, various orders from South Africa for wagons, carriages and tramcars must have been very welcome. This splendid all metal lightweight double-deck tramcar would make a fine sight rattling through Johannesburg. *Author's collection*

49

SOUTH AFRICAN RAILWAYS & HARBOURS
3ft 6" GAUGE
FIRST CLASS STEEL AIR CONDITIONED MAIN LINE COACH TYPE "B"
TO SEAT 11 PASSENGERS
CONTRACT NO. 2/1/2679.

LENGTH OVER VESTIBULE BUFFERS   67' 6"   CENTRES OF BOGIES   42' 6"
LENGTH OVER HEADSTOCKS   63' 5"   BOGIE WHEELBASE   6' 6"
WIDTH OVER SIDE PANELS ABOVE WAIST   9' 3¾"   DIA. OF WHEELS   2' 10"
HEIGHT FROM RAIL   12' 9⅝"

TARE WEIGHT 43 TONS 4 CWTS. 2 QRS.
NO WATER IN TANKS.

BUILT BY METROPOLITAN-CAMMELL CARRIAGE & WAGON CO. LTD.
ENGLAND
1939
H.O. 7758   NEG. NO. 7950

A first class air conditioned coach built in 1939 for South African Railways 12-coach prestigious train the 'Union Limited'. In 1946 the 'Union Limited' was renamed the 'Blue Train'.

Author's collection

50

THE DENABY & CADEBY MAIN COLLIERIES LTD.
12 TON COAL WAGON

LENGTH OVER HEADSTOCKS	16' 8"	WIDTH INSIDE BODY 7' 6¼"
LENGTH INSIDE BODY	16' 0¼"	HEIGHT INSIDE BODY 4' 7¾"
JOURNALS	9" x 4¼"	CAPACITY CUBIC FEET 550

BUILT BY METROPOLITAN-CAMMELL CARRIAGE & WAGON CO. LTD.
MIDLAND WORKS, ENGLAND.
1935.
HO. 5436
NEG. NO. 9280.

Private owner wagons brought some variety to long trains of coal, although it is unlikely that this example, built at the Midland Works in 1935, stayed in pristine condition for very long. Maltby was in the South Yorkshire coalfield and the wagon carries an 'LNER-E' registration plate which authorises main line running.

Author's collection

51

Metropolitan-Cammell customers, 1929-45

Andalucia (Pullmans) (1929)	Buenos Aires Midland (1934)	Dorado (Columbia) (1936)	Tramways (1934/36)
Anglo-Iranian Oil Co (1937)	Central Argentine (1930)	Edinburgh Corporation Tramways	Kalighat-Falta (India)
Assan Railway & Trading Co	Central of Brazil (1937)	(1934/5)	Kenya & Uganda (1929-41)
(1937)	Central Uruguay (1929)	Egyptian State (1942/3)	Leopoldina (1944/5)
Bengal & North Western (1932/7)	Ceylon Government (1929/32/44)	Great Western of Brazil (1937/8)	Lobito Oilfields (1935)
Benguela (various)	Cordoba Central (1930)	Johannesburg Municipal	LMSR (1929,1933-8)

Leeds Forge-Orders for Underframes

Argentine,	British Honduras,	Dublin & South Eastern,	Lancashire Derbyshire &
Assam Bengal,	Caledonian,	East Indian,	East Coast,
Barry,	Central Argentine	Eastern Bengal,	Leek & Manifold,
Barsi Light Rly,	Central Cordoba,	Indian State Railways,	Madras-Cochin,
Bengal-Nagpur,	Central South Africa,	Koivista-Forssa (Finland)	Midland Great Western,
Bezwada-Madras,	Cyprus Government,	Kowloon-Canton,	Oudh & Rohilkund,
Bridgetown & St Andrews	Darjeeling Himalayan,	Lagos Steam Tramway,	New South Wales Government,
(Barbados),	Demerara,		South Indian

A notable order for underframes came from the Central Argentine Railway. Twin cars, consisting of a first class unit and a kitchen/restaurant unit, were built on six-wheel Gresley articulated bogies, said at the time to be the longest and heaviest vehicles ever built on this system of articulation. They were in service in 1928 on the Rosario Express.

Leeds Forge Co Ltd. (Newlay Carriage Works opened 1908) Principal rail transport customers, 1908 to 1928

Barsi Light Railway (1925)	Tramways(1923-built at Bristol)	Mogyana Railway (1908)	Ugandan (1925)
Buenos Aires Great Southern	Federated Malay States Railways	New South Wales Government	Underground Group
(1923)	(1908)	(1926)	(Bakerloo, District, bogies 1914)
East Indian (1926)	Honduras (1909)	Nilgiri (1914)	Vascongados (Spain),
Edinburgh Corporation	Kalka-Simla Railway (1910)	South Indian (1925)	(1928 Pullman)
Egyptian State Railways 1928	Kowloon-Canton(1925)	Sudan Government (1909)	Wagons Lits (1922, 1927)

The principal Leeds Forge works at Armley produced (inter alia) pressed steel wagons, locomotive tenders and steel underframes.

Midland Railway-Carriage & Wagon Co Ltd customers. (Washwood Heath works opened 1912)

Pullman Car Co, 1922	Manchester South Junction &	Services) (1932)	South African (1935-9)
Pullman Car Co, 1922 (for LMS)	Altrincham (1930/1)	Ransomes & Rapier (match	South Indian (1929)
Pullman Car Co, Wagons Lits	Ministry of Supply (Wagons for	wagons) (1930 Malaya)	Sudan Government (1930)
(1928)	France) (1939/40)	Rhodesia (various)	Tanganyika (1929)
LNER (Tyneside) (1937/8)	Nigerian (1934/5)	Roumanian State Railways (1932)	Trans-Zambesi (1939)
London Underground Group	Nizam of Hyderabad (1932/5/9)	Sao Paulo (1936-40)	US Government (1942/3)
(1930/1)	Nyasaland (1939)	Shanghai-Nanking (1936)	Wagons Lits (1929)
London Transport (1936-40)	Pullman Car Co (Southern Electric	Southern (1932-7)	

An interesting vehicle built in 1927 was a bogie Dynamometer Car for the Buenos Aires Great Southern Railway, described in the trade press as 'probably one of the most up-to-date vehicles of this class yet produced.' It was 62' long over the buffers and contained seven compartments comprising test room, saloon, three bedrooms, kitchen and bathroom. The outside body was varnished teak, while the inside had polished mahogany. The saloon featured an ornamental fireplace! Some of the measuring instruments in the test room were specially developed by the Midland Railway-Carriage and Wagon Co to give accurate technical details of a locomotive's performance and coal and water consumption under test conditions.

No official Midland works list for the period from 1912 to 1928 has been traced. Some earlier orders feature in Birmingham Central Library's list of microfiche drawings.

CHAPTER 7

Metro-Cammell at War 1939-1945

Long before war was declared many of Britain's military men had become increasingly alarmed about Germany's build up of arms and our lack of modern fighting equipment to counter the threat.

Although a War Office policy for updating our armaments was formulated in 1936, matters didn't come to a head until about the time of the Munich crisis in 1938. Then, along with other manufacturers, Metro-Cammell was asked to supply military equipment by the War Office.

Metro's first contract was for 45 A10 'Cruiser' tanks carrying a 2 pounder gun. This was followed in the spring of 1939 by 30 A10 'Cruiser' close support tanks carrying 3.7 mortar mountings, Vickers-Armstrong Ltd, the parent of the A10 supplying the manufacturing information. The contract was allotted to the Old Park works, Wednesbury, the first tank being completed for testing and trial running in December 1939. The last of 75 machines which were ordered were delivered in September 1940.

In May 1939, Metro-Cammell were asked to undertake production of 'Valentine' tanks, again under the parentage of Vickers-Armstrong, but at that time only outline drawings and a wooden mock up were available. The contract for 125 of these machines was received from the War Office in July 1939, but it was not expected to start delivery until twelve months later. The first completed machine was despatched from Old Park works at the end of July 1940.

Subsequent contracts for 'Valentines', up to a total of 2,135, were placed and were divided between the Midland and Old Park works, which attained a maximum monthly output of 82 in July 1942. Many improvements were effected in the 'Valentine' during the course of 3 1/2 years of continuous output, including the replacement of 2-pdr. by 6-pdr. guns, and eventually by 75 mm. guns. A number of these tanks were supplied and hulls adapted for fitting elsewhere with 'Scissor' bridges. However, the most interesting development on 'Valentines' was the conversion of 625 into amphibious tanks, of which more later.

Although the 'Valentines' were superseded by heavier and faster tanks, favourable reports were received as to their reliability under operational conditions. What the Wellington bomber was to the R.A.F., the 'Valentine' was to the Army. Both did most valiant service at a time when this country stood alone. The need of fighting tanks became acute after Dunkirk. Consequently, Metro-Cammell were asked by the Ministry of Supply to participate in the building of the new heavy infantry tanks, the 'Churchill'. In August 1940, only a wooden mock-up of this machine was available, but the first 'Churchill' to be completed at Old Park works - where assembly of this type proceeded concurrently with 'Valentine' production- was delivered early in July 1941.

Further 'Churchill' contracts were received up to a total of 435, and the later contracts covered many improvements,

including 6-pdr. instead of 2-pdr. gun mountings and substitutions of cast turrets by welded turrets. Regular weekly output of these assemblies was maintained until completion of the contracts in September 1943.

The works also supplied 185 hull assemblies for building into complete tanks by other firms and in addition re-armoured a large number of 'Churchills'.

Having previously undertaken production of four other types of fighting tanks, yet again the company was asked by the Ministry of Supply, in December 1941, to provide capacity for a new type of heavy cruiser tank – the 'Cromwell'. The first contract for 275 of these machines was received in February 1942 followed in December of that year by two further contracts, each for 300 'Cromwells', making a total of 875. Subsequently these contracts were revised to provide for the supply of 50 'Cromwells' with 6-pdr. guns, 299 close support 'Cromwells' fitted with 95mm. guns and 325 'Comets' – an improved type developed from 'Cromwells' – fitted with 77mm. high velocity guns. Production of 274 'Cromwells' and 325 'Comets' was allotted to the Midland Works, and '75 Cromwells' to Old Park works.

Delivery of 95mm. 'Cromwells' was first made from the former factory at the end of July 1943, and although, owing to design modifications, output proceeded somewhat slowly during the remainder of that year, the rate increased early in 1944 and 100 of these machines had been delivered by D-Day.

'Cromwells' were completed at the rate of one each day for the remainder of that year, towards the end of which 'Comets' were also being delivered. These fast tanks, fitted with Rolls-Royce engines, and equipped with heavier calibre guns than those on earlier types, were reported to have given splendid service in the final campaigns of the European war. When the war ended contracts were terminated with the completion of 300 'Cromwells' and 150 'Comets'.

Small numbers of two types of light tanks were built in the Midland Works. The 'Tetrarch', fitted with a 2-pdr. gun was the first – though it was delayed in production – one serious setback resulting from destruction of a number of engines in the factory by enemy bombs. The last of these machines was completed in March 1942. This was the type chosen for airborne conveyance by Horsa gliders.

Also built were 102 'Harry Hopkins' light tanks, fitted with 2-pdr. and Besa co-axial gun mountings. Production of this machine, adapted as a 95 mm. SP gun carrier to suit the changed conditions for later military campaigns, was then transferred to Vickers-Armstrong.

One of the most remarkable of the many ingenious new devices produced during the war was the amphibious fighting tank known as the 'Swimming' tank and Metro-Cammell was selected to develop and put into quantitative production in its Midland works (under conditions of strictest secrecy) the inventor's design for machines of this type.

Above: Valentine tanks undergoing test manoeuvres.

Tank Museum Collection

Below: The Cromwell tank carried a crew of five and, despite its weight of nearly 30 tons, it could top 18mph across country thanks to its powerful 600hp Rolls-Royce Meteor engines. The main armament varied between 6pdr, 75mm and 95mm guns although an improved version, the Comet, carried 77mm high velocity canon.

Author's collection

Briefly the invention involved the fitting of steel decking on the top of the tank hull and flotation equipment in the shape of a canvas screen attached to the deckline and raised by rubber columns (later supplemented by mechanical struts) inflated by air under pressure. Propulsion through water was derived from propellers fitted outside the tank and driven from its engine. When the screen was dropped on emerging from the water, the tank would immediately resume its normal function as a land fighting machine.

After successful trials had been carried out on a 'Tetrarch' converted by the inventor, a contract was placed in July 1942, for conversion of 450 (subsequently increased to 625) 'Valentine' tanks fitted with similar but larger and heavier equipment. With the exception of three pilot models, the tanks were to be taken from the 'Valentine' production line for conversion.

The task involved the solution of many complicated technical and production problems. A secluded pool was found and provided with concrete runway, etc., which necessitated the engagement of a skilled diver and the placating of the farmer who didn't want his cows poisoned by 'they contraptions'. Each converted machine was taken there for testing for serviceability, not only in flotation and propulsion but also in manoeuvrability, water-tightness, etc. Trials also had to be carried out with prototypes by the Army, first at fresh water sites and later in the sea under conditions closely approximating to those likely to be met in actual landing operations.

The first sea trials took place in August 1942, at pre-selected points on the English coasts. An intrepid member of Metro-Cammell's technical staff, as well as one from the inventor's firm, were included in the crew, and they were able to obtain first-hand experience of the results achieved.

The job aroused great interest amongst the technical staff and work people, by whom the problems were tackled energetically and enthusiastically as they arose, and a most cordial spirit of co-operation was established with the inventor's firm, Army authorities, Ministry of Supply officials and Combined Operations Staff. The trials and experimental stage necessarily occupied several months.

Delivery of Duplex Drive 'Valentines' (as these amphibious machines were then designated) began at the beginning of March 1943. By the end of 1943, 378 of these 'swimmers' had been completed, and the remaining 247 in the following year. Many of these DD 'Valentines' were used for training amphibious tank crews in this country.

Meanwhile, however, the company had been asked to convert, in the same way, 573 American 'Sherman' tanks, which again involved the solution of many new problems, as this machine, equipped with a 75mm. gun, weighed 34 tons compared with about 17 tons in the case of the 'Valentine'. Prototypes of the DD conversion of this machine also had to be prepared and tried out first at fresh water sites and subsequently in the sea.

Great efforts were required to produce these machines in time for the invasion of Europe. On D-Day numbers of these amphibious 'Shermans' were used with conspicuous success and provided the necessary tank support which was such a vital requirement immediately following the landing of the infantry. Similarly, machines of this type were subsequently used in crossing the Rhine, a feat successfully achieved against the strong currents of that fast-flowing river.

Although actual tank building was not carried out at the Saltley works, a vital contribution to tank output was made from there by the constant supply of forgings and stampings from the smithy, and the machining of many thousands of these parts, including large quantities of spares.

Saltley works had the distinction of being the leading source of supply of Radar vehicle bodies and associated mechanical equipment throughout the war period. It was in the Radar 'picture' in the early days of its development, the first contract from the Ministry of Supply having been received in October 1939, for 50 Mark 1 Receiver-type Cabins. Delivery began in March 1940, and by that time a further contract for the same type has already been placed. Many of these earlier cabins were used in the Battle of Britain.

A few months later, contracts for 650 each Mark II Receiver and Transmitter-type Cabins were received and deliveries followed closely after completion of the first two contracts. By the end of 1941, 1,150 Radar vehicles had been delivered. Meanwhile there had been vast expansion in use of Radar and in September 1941 a contract was received for the designing and building of 550 steel-bodied vehicles of an improved type (Mark III). Many were delivered during the following year, as well as production of a special mobile type fitted with parabolic reflectors. As model succeeded model the design of the accompanying aerial structures became increasingly intricate and unique problems had to be met, due to their great size and the importance of accurate conformity in the parabolic curves (the works called them 'elephant ears'). In all this development close liaison was kept with the research establishments of Air Defence, Admirality Signals, and the RAF., and types were developed to meet the ever-changing needs of modern warfare, including the problems of D-Day and the widespread conflict in the Far East. The total number of Radar vehicles of various types built at Saltley was nearly 3,000.

Although still heavily engaged on tank building, in August 1944, the company was asked to undertake production of a new vehicle-cum-craft under the parentage of Morris Motors Ltd. Machines of this type, called 'Neptune' freight carriers, were expected to be used in operations against the Japanese for landing military supplies, and then reverting to operation as tracked vehicles. Experience in making 'swimming' tanks provided valuable assistance in this new project. The sudden collapse of the Japanese, following the dropping of the atomic bombs, resulted in the termination of the 'Neptune' contract when 70 of these vehicles had been completed at the Midland works and 105 hulls for assembly at Old Park.

In 1941 production of hulls and turrets was started for assembly into complete armoured cars by motor car manufacturers. Constant output of these was maintained from the Midland works for the next three years, reaching a total of 2,600 complete hulls with turrets and 2,800 separate turrets.

With 90 per cent of capacity diverted to armament production manufacture of railway wagons, from 1940 onwards, was on a very limited scale, but output included 800 bogie flat wagons for carrying fighting tanks, about 1,000 wagons for carrying iron ore and a number of aviations spirit tank wagons on which heavy calibre mobile guns were to be mounted. Other orders were wagons for the Ministry of Supply, flat cars for the US Army, and later wagons for Egypt, Kenya and Ceylon.

3,600 25-pdr. artillery trailers were supplied during the three years ending 1943. Large numbers of components for military bridging equipment were also manufactured, as well as parts for the Mulbury Harbour.

Although most of the war contracts emanated from the Ministry of Supply, there were some from the Admiralty, 950 Multiple Rocket Projectile mountings, commonly called 'Pillar Boxes' and 'Blunderbusses', and many thousands of shackles for

Above: Over 100 of these lightweight 'Harry Hopkins' tanks were built by Metro-Cammell. They were named in honour of US President Roosevelt's wartime assistant who personally gave great help to Britain in the darker days of the war, in particular, administrating the lend-lease of goods and military equipment from America. *Author's collection*

War time Ministry of Supply order for 16 ton all-steel mineral wagons with side and end doors. This one was registered for use by the L.M.S. *B.J.R. Yates*

M.W.T 3001
16 TONS

MINISTRY OF SUPPLY
CONTRACT NO. 294/27/5743 (CON.27.B1)
16 TON ALL STEEL MINERAL WAGON

MINISTRY OF SUPPLY
CONTRACT NO. 294/43/P/3611/CON.23B.
RADAR VEHICLE TYPE 461
Built by
METROPOLITAN-CAMMELL CARRIAGE & WAGON CO. LTD.,
1944
HO.10577.   NEG. NO. 8094.

The special mobile radar cabin and its parabolic reflector mounted on the chassis of a six wheel Bedford Lorry in 1944. The reflector, aptly nicknamed 'elephant ears', could be 'finely tuned' by means of a long rod fitted to a crank from a reduction box and electric motor seen in the picture.

Author's collection

boom defences. As sub-contractors to shipbuilders, 164 pre-fabricated hull sections for tugs and light tankers were also completed.

Throughout the war there were many distinguished visitors, amongst whom were the Duke and Duchess of Gloucester, Field-Marshall The Right Hon. J.C. Smuts, Sir Andrew Duncan, then Minister of Supply, and M Maisky. Many 'Top Secret' conferences were held at the Works, particularly in connection with swimming tank contracts. For one conference, attended by some of the highest-ranking officers of the War Office General Staff, a special train from London was bought direct into the Midland works; the display of ribbons and gold braid must have been terrific! Another visit was that made by '

Monty', not long before the invasion of Europe was to begin and his 'pep' talk added even greater incentive to the strenuous endeavours already being made by the personnel to play their part in what proved to be the most glorious military achievement in history. He also congratulated a Guard of Honour mounted by picked representatives of the two Home Guard Companies raised by the Works.

Saltley and the Midland works both situated in one of the most vulnerable target areas of Birmingham were each on the receiving end of German bombers during the war, over 100 HE bombs dropping within their boundaries on different occasions in addition to many oil and incendiary devices.

Saltley suffered the most with the whole of the Drawing Office block being destroyed in one of the early air raids in October, 1940, the ensuing fire consuming valuable records and equipment, necessitating the rehousing of the Drawing Office, Estimating, Buying Department and Accountancy staff. Whilst waiting to be rehoused, BRCW came partly to the rescue in providing the Drawing Office staff with temporary accommodation and facilities at their Smethwick factory, whilst over 40 vital engineering staff were temporarily billeted away from the 'war zone' at the 'Nautical William Hotel', near Bridgnorth, Shropshire.

In April 1941, the Saw Mill at Saltley, regarded as one of the finest in the country, was destroyed and heavy damage was suffered by the Midland works on the same night. However, the workforce resolutely soldiered on in the face of adversity with a determination to 'keep the wheels turning'. Fortunately, the Old Park works and adjacent steel plant of The Patent Shaft and Axletree Co. at Wednesbury, remained unscathed throughout the war.

As the tide began to turn, in 1944, towards an Allied victory, moves were already taking place to restore peace time normality. The Pullman Car Company had arranged for some of its temporarily unemployed cars to be stored on Metropolitan sidings, ready to move into the works for refurbishment, once the war was over and men and materials became available. These cars were eventually used on the new *Devon Belle* in 1947.

Meanwhile, there could still be no relaxation for the work force until the last 'all clear' was sounded, and when it did, on 7 May 1945, the company was the largest supplier of tanks in the UK, its managing director Mr A. J. Boyd also being director-general of tank production at the Ministry of Supply. Everyone involved with the war effort could justifiably be proud of the part they played in the victory.

Sadly, Frank Dudley Docker, for nearly 28 years the guiding hand of the largest rolling stock maker in Britain, wasn't there to share in the celebrations or witness the company's first century in business, for he had died, peacefully, on 8 July 1944 at his home in Amersham aged 81 years.

1939-1945 Wartime Production

TANKS

No.	Type	Armament	
45	A10	2 pdr	
30	A10	3.7 mortar	
1545	Valentine	2 pdr	625 converted
460	Valentine	6 pdr	to amphibious
130	Valentine	75mm	tanks
435	Churchill	2 & 6 pdr	
573	Sherman (USA origin)	converted to amphibious tanks	
50	Cromwell	6 pdr	
135	Cromwell	75mm	
115	Cromwell	95mm	
150	Comet	95mm	
100	Tetrarch (Mark VII)	2 pdr	
102	Harry Hopkins	2 pdr	

OTHER VEHICLES AND MILITARY EQUIPMENT

1250	Radar receiver and transmitter cabins
70	Neptune landing vehicles
2600	Armoured cars
800	Tank carrier bogie wagons
3600	Artillery trailers for 25 pdr shells
950	Multiple rocket projector mountings

The Post-War Years
1946-1962

Metro-Cammell ended the 1939-45 War with a backlog of demand that promised several years of steady work. At Government request, priority was given to exports, and large wagon orders were fulfilled for Argentina, Burma, Malaya, Nigeria, Rhodesia and South Africa, mostly placed as usual by the Crown Agents, whose inspectors were frequent visitors to the works. When an Open Day was held at Saltley works on 17 June 1950, visitors could see coaches being built for British Railways and for South Africa, and wagons for Nigeria, East Africa and Turkey. A 12-car-train was built at Old Park works for the 1947 Royal Tour of South Africa, and an official model of one coach is in the Birmingham Museum of Science and Industry. A notable British contract (shared with BRCW) was for 92 Liverpool Street-Shenfield and eight Manchester-Glossop electric trains for British Railways. Electric welding for bodywork was now general, but British industry did not follow the American trend towards building in stainless steel.

One of the most unusual repeat orders came in 1950 from the Egyptian State Railways. Between 1925 and 1933 Cammell Laird and Metro-Cammell had built 80 Sentinel-Cammell steam railcars for the LNER, and nearly as many again for other companies and for export. The last LNER car was withdrawn in 1948, but two years later the Egyptian State Railways placed an order for ten three-car Sentinel steam railcar sets. At first sight

Metro-Cammell Head Production Drawing Office, Saltley Works, Birmingham in September 1949. Staff at this time numbered about 70 men. In addition, there were 25 rail car drawing office staff, 10 stress office staff and 35 tracing office staff giving a grand total of 140.

B.J.R. Yates

CENTRAL RAILWAY OF BRAZIL
SECOND CLASS STEEL TRAILER COACH
5' 3" Gauge

Length over Headstocks 68'7.7/16"(20000 m/m)   Centres of Bogies 45'11.3/16"(14000 m/m)
Width over Body Panels   9'9.3/16"(2976 m/m)   Bogie Wheelbase   8' 0"   (2438 m/m)
Height from Rail to Top 12' 9.9/16"(3900 m/m)   Seating Accommodation   72
      of Roof   Standing Accommodation   148

Tare Weight 34 Tons. 14 Cwts.

HO.13062.   Built by METROPOLITAN-CAMMELL CARRIAGE & WAGON CO.LTD.,
                                          ENGLAND
                                            1947
                                                            NEG. NO. 6204

1947-built second class trailer coach for the Central Railway of Brazil, part of an order for 30 three-car electric units. Each car could accommodate 220 passengers, 72 seated and 148 standing! A later 1955/6 batch with strengthened under frames, was capable of carrying up to 400 passengers, over 320 of those standing.

Author's collection

Above: The 12 coach royal train was built in 1946 by the Old Park works of Metro-Cammell for the 1947 royal tour of South Africa. It is seen at a specially built staging site near East London, Cape Province in 1947. After the tour, most of the cars were used to form a second 'Blue Train'. *Author's collection*

Below: From 1935 Metro-Cammell supplied most of the electric multiple unit stock for South Africa's suburban lines around Johannesburg and Cape Town. Pictured is a 1948 built third class motor coach for the high-density lines around Johannesburg and Pretoria known as the Reef. These coaches had a high carrying capacity 90 seats which was often exceeded at peak times! *Author's collection*

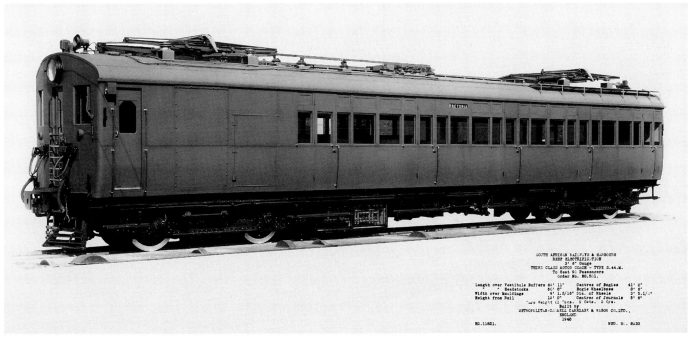

SOUTH AFRICAN RAILWAYS & HARBOURS
REEF ELECTRIFICATION
3' 6" Gauge
THIRD CLASS MOTOR COACH - TYPE S.44.M.
To Seat 90 Passengers
Order No. NS.501.

Length over Vestibule Buffers	64' 11"	Centres of Bogies	41' 0"
" " Headstocks	60' 6"	Bogie Wheelbase	8' 6"
Width over Mouldings	9' 1.3/16"	Dia. of Wheels	3' 5.1/2"
Height from Rail	12' 0"	Centres of Journals	5' 6"
Tare Weight (1 Tons. 9 Cwts. 2 Qrs.			

Built by
METROPOLITAN-CAMMELL CARRIAGE & WAGON CO.LTD.,
ENGLAND
1948

NO.11851.   NEG. NO. 8233

REPUBLICA ARGENTINA — FERROCARRIL
NACIONAL — GENERAL SAN MARTIN.

50 TON BOGIE COVERED WAGON.

Length over Buffers	..	41' 4"	Width inside	9' 11½"
Length over Headstocks		38' 0"	Clear Height inside ..	8' 10"
Centres of Bogies	..	25' 0"	Maximum Height from rail	12' 9½"
Bogie Wheelbase	..	6' 0"	Size of Journal ..	10' x 5½"

Load 50 Tons. Tare 20 Tons. 4 Cwts.

Built by
METROPOLITAN-CAMMELL CARRIAGE AND WAGON CO. LTD.
ENGLAND.
Consulting Engineers : FOX & MAYO, LONDON, E.C.2.
1949.

H.O. 14368.   NEG. No. 8308A

Above: A 1949 50 ton bogie covered wagon built for Argentine Railways.   *Author's collection*

Below: Nigerian Railways 3' 6" gauge bogie goods brake van of 1949.   *Author's collection*

NIGERIAN RAILWAY
3' 6" Gauge
PECN. NO. 300/1 & 785/3
BOGIE GOODS BRAKE VAN

Length over Headstocks 31' 0"	Bogie Wheelbase 5' 6"
Width over Corner Pillars 7' 8"	Height to Top of Roof 11' 0.1/4"
Bogie Centre 21' 0"	Journals 7.1/4" x 3.9/16"

Tare Weight Tons 11. 17. 0. 12.

Built by
METROPOLITAN-CAMMELL CARRIAGE & WAGON CO.,LTD.,
ENGLAND
1949

HO.14552.   Neg. No. 8294

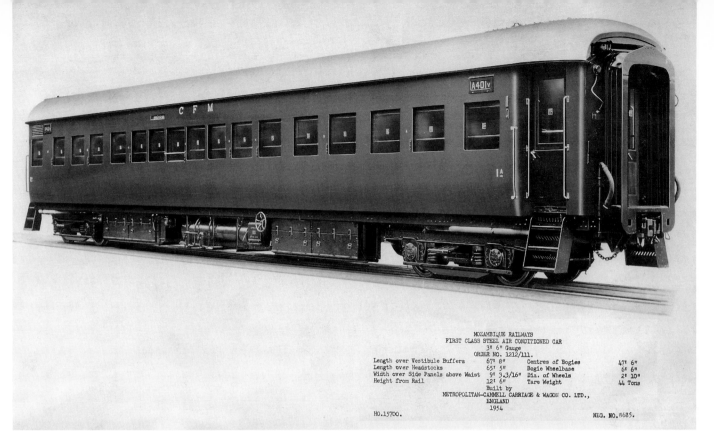

MOZAMBIQUE RAILWAYS
FIRST CLASS STEEL AIR CONDITIONED CAR
3' 6" Gauge
ORDER NO. 1212/111.

Length over Vestibule Buffers	67' 8"	Centres of Bogies	47' 6"
Length over Headstocks	65' 5"	Bogie Wheelbase	6' 6"
Width over Side Panels above Waist	9' 3.3/16"	Dia. of Wheels	2' 10"
Height from Rail	12' 6"	Tare Weight	44 Tons

Built by
METROPOLITAN-CAMMELL CARRIAGE & WAGON CO. LTD.,
ENGLAND
1954

HO.15700.   NEG. NO. 8685.

MOZAMBIQUE RAILWAYS
FIRST CLASS STEEL AIR CONDITIONED CAR
ORDER NO. 1212/111.
Built by
METROPOLITAN-CAMMELL CARRIAGE & WAGON CO. LTD.,
ENGLAND
1954
HO.15700.   NEG.NO.8692.

Above: 1st class steel air conditioned carriage for the 3' 6" gauge Beira system of Mozambique Railways. One of five 1st class and eight 2nd class coaches ordered by the Portuguese government in 1950 for their colony in East Africa. This particular vehicle was delivered in 1954.   *Author's collection*

Left: The interior of a 1st class compartment. Note the veneer panelling and wash basin neatly stowed away.   *Author's collection*

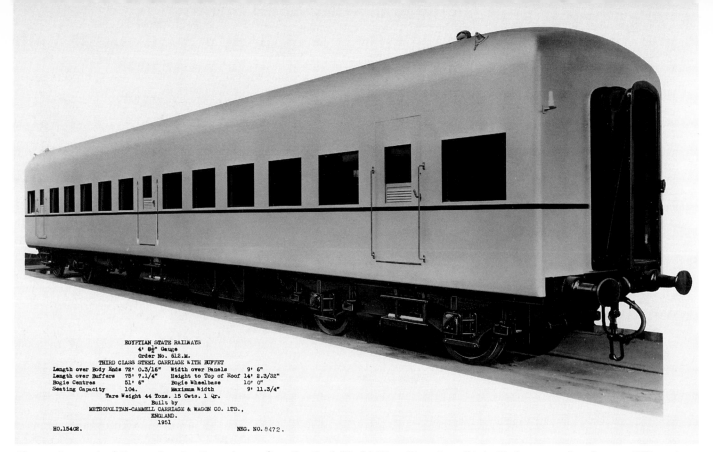

EGYPTIAN STATE RAILWAYS
4' 8½" Gauge
Order No. 612.M.
THIRD CLASS STEEL CARRIAGE WITH BUFFET

Length over Body Ends	72' 0.3/16"	Width over Panels	9' 6"
Length over Buffers	75' 7.1/4"	Height to Top of Roof	14' 2.3/32"
Bogie Centres	51' 6"	Bogie Wheelbase	10' 0"
Seating Capacity	104.	Maximum Width	9' 11.3/4"

Tare Weight 44 Tons. 15 Cwts. 1 Qr.
Built by
METROPOLITAN-CAMMELL CARRIAGE & WAGON CO. LTD.,
ENGLAND.
1951
HO.15402.   NEG. NO.8472.

Above: As part of its modernisation plan, after the 2nd World War, Egyptian State Railways ordered over 180 various carriages between 1946 and 1951. The example built in 1951 is a 3rd class, all-steel carriage with buffet. *Author's collection*

Below: The interior of the very spartan 3rd class carriage with the buffet area at the far end. Although fitted with electric lights, the glass globes are more reminiscent of gas lighting once fitted to older British stock! *Author's collection*

EGYPTIAN STATE RAILWAYS
4' 8½" Gauge
Order No. 612.M.
THIRD CLASS STEEL CARRIAGE WITH BUFFET
Built by
METROPOLITAN-CAMMELL CARRIAGE & WAGON CO. LTD.,
ENGLAND.
1951
HO.15402.   NEG. NO.8473.

QUEENSLAND GOVERNMENT RAILWAYS
FOUR-WHEELED OPEN LOWSIDED WAGON TYPE "F.J.S"
3' 6" Gauge

Length over Headstocks	17' 6"	Total Height from Rail	5' 8.11/16"
Width inside Body	7'10.1/2"	Wheelbase	10' 6"
Height inside body at sides	2' 7.1/2"	Journals	8" x 4"

Tare Weight 5 Tons. 10 Cwts. 3 Qrs.
Built by
METROPOLITAN-CAMMELL CARRIAGE & WAGON CO. LTD.,
ENGLAND
.1953

HO.15979.   NEG. NO. 8663.

Above: Queensland Government Railways 4-wheeled open low-sided wagon built for 3' 6" gauge in 1953.   *Author's collection*

Below: Refrigerated wagon bodies and underframes leaving Saltley works in 1958 for shipment to New Zealand, where, on arrival, they would be united with their 3' 6" gauge bogies. 100 of these wagons were sent to New Zealand, those pictured being fitted for chilled beef which was unusual given the sheep population! Refrigeration was obtained by packing compartments with crushed ice via manhole covers on the roof.   *Author's collection*

BRITISH RAILWAYS
LONDON MIDLAND REGION
21-TON ALL STEEL MINERAL WAGON
LOT NO. 2190

Length over Headstocks	21' 6"	Wheelbase	12' 0"
Overall Height	9' 1"	Size of Journals	10" x 5"
Width Inside	7' 11.1/2"	Diameter of Wheels on Tread	3' 1.1/2"
Buffer Height	3' 5"	Capacity	21·24 Tons

Built by
METROPOLITAN-CAMMELL CARRIAGE & WAGON CO. LTD.,
ENGLAND
1951

HO.15480.   NEG. NO. 8416

Above: Metro-Cammell supplied British Railways with a thousand of these 21 ton all-steel mineral wagons. This one was destined for the London Midland Region in 1951.   *Author's collection*

Below: 25 ton self-discharging hopper ballast wagon for British Railways Eastern & North Eastern Regions in 1951. These were identical to others supplied to the L.N.E.R. just prior to nationalisation in 1948.   *Author's collection*

BRITISH RAILWAYS
EASTERN & NORTH EASTERN REGIONS
SELF DISCHARGING HOPPER BALLAST WAGON
LOT NO. 2188

Length over Headstocks	21' 2"	Wheelbase	12' 6"
Length inside Body	18' 0.1/2"	Gauge	4' 8.1/2"
Width inside Body	8' 2"	Capacity of Wagon	25 Tons

Built by
METROPOLITAN-CAMMELL CARRIAGE & WAGON CO. LTD.,
ENGLAND
1951

HO.15458.   NEG. NO.6

these could easily have been mistaken for diesels, except for the exhaust. They entered service in 1951/2 between Cairo and Helwan, and were transferred to the Delta after the Helwan line's electrification, being withdrawn and stored by 1964. One set has been repatriated by the Buckingham Railway Centre and is now at Quainton Road. Finally two more steam railcars were supplied to the Nigerian State Railways in 1953, the last steam railcars to be built in England.

The 1950s heralded a change in carriage building, from steel body work to aluminium, a milestone as important as that from timber to steel, and Metro-Cammell, together with London Transport, were the leaders. The first extensive use of aluminium panelled cars for London Transport, were 90 surface cars (District Line R49 stock) built by Metro-Cammell over the period 1951-53. Each car weighed 28 tons, a saving of nearly 6 tons over the steel variety, and one of these cars was exhibited at the 1951 Festival of Britain.

Although the cost of the aluminium bodied cars was higher than the steel ones, London Transport tests found lower energy and maintenance savings which, over a period of time, would offset the initial outlay, so much so, that in 1957-58, 3 new, seven car aluminium panelled tube trains (1956 stock) were placed on trial on the Piccadilly Line. These trains were delivered from the makers, Metro-Cammell, Gloucester Railway Carriage, and BRCW, unpainted, unlike the original aluminium R49 stock which was, but later had the paint removed.

As a result of these trials Metro-Cammell received large orders, over a period of years, to re-equip the Piccadilly, Northern, Circle, Central and Metropolitan lines, and it is interesting to note that BRs Derby Works, which was also using aluminium in its lightweight diesel railcars, shared the Central line contract with Metro-Cammell.

In 1956 BR ordered 24 three-car sets for the electrified Mersey rail network, comprising a motor car, a composite trailer and driving trailer. The motor cars were built by Metro-Cammell, while the composites were shared between Metro-Cammell and BRCW, the latter also building the driving trailers. Export orders for passenger stock in the late 1950s and early 1960s included 30 more three-car electric suburban trains for the Central Railway of Brazil, 23 coaches for the Kowloon-Canton Railway, 20 railcars for Jamaica, coaches for Egypt, multiple-unit stock for South Africa, and electric trains for Calcutta and Bombay. In the Indian trains, the floors and the lower side panels were wine red, to conceal stains from betel-nut juice!

After a long absence the company re-entered the field of locomotive manufacture, with an order for 1000hp diesel electric locomotives for New South Wales in conjunction with BTH. This was followed by 94 Crossley-engined diesel locomotives for Ireland with AEI as main contractor. This order at the time represented the largest to be placed for diesel electrics with a private contractor in the UK. AEI or GEC-powered electric locomotives were also supplied for South Africa and Pakistan. From 1961 onwards electric trains, and mainline

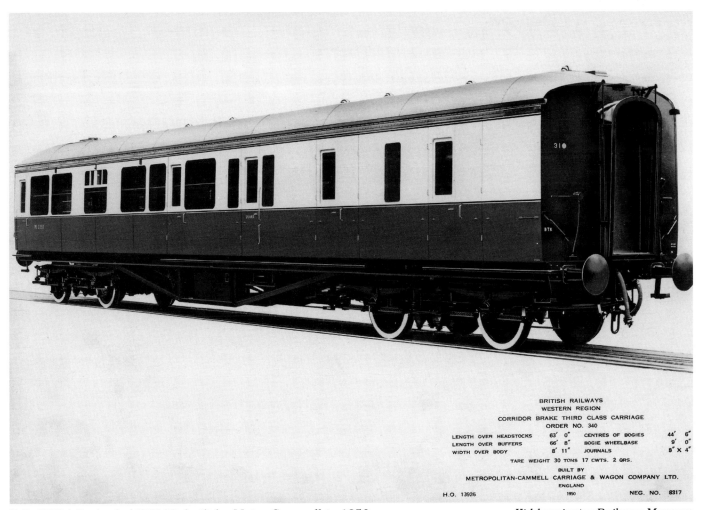

BR. (W.R.) Brake 3rd W2138, built by Metro-Cammell in 1950.   *Kidderminster Railway Museum*

The British Railways modernisation programme of the 1950s included the construction of large numbers of diesel multiple units (DMUs) and Metro-Cammell were heavily involved. In 1955 the firm produced thirty-six 2-car 'lightweight' sets for BR. From 1956 onwards Metro built a big series of no less than 637 DMU vehicles, with their distinctive design. Although the earlier 'lightweight' series were all withdrawn by the end of the 1960s, the main series were, by common consent, very successful and some have been in service for over forty years.

Above: Motor brake second Sc51237 heads two shiny new DMUs posing for an official photograph dated 21 May 1958.

Kidderminster Railway Museum

Below: Trailer brake second NE59093 was part of a 4-car set when seen at Leeds Neville Hill on 8 October 1967.   *D Percival*

The 'Wirral' trains for the Mersey Tunnel Services were built by Metro-Cammell and B.R.C.W. in 1937/8 with a further batch in 1956/7 of which M28379M is one. These trains had Alpax aluminium alloy doors and window frames. *B.J.R. Yates*

carriages to Metro-Cammell designs, were built in South Africa by Union Carriage & Wagon Co (Pty) Ltd, in which Metro-Cammell had an interest.

In the late 1950s, much of the workload, apart from underground stock, was provided by British Railways' 1955 Modernisation Plan, under which Metro-Cammell supplied over 1,300 Mark 1 coaches and no fewer than 760 diesel railcars, many of which outlasted those built by other firms. (Metro's first order for Mark 1 coaches was received from British Railways in 1951. The contract called for construction of 206 first and third class composite corridor coaches and 20 first and third class brake composite corridor coaches.) The company also built the five diesel-electric *Blue Pullman* trains of 1959 (BR's first air-conditioned stock) and the 44 East Coast Pullmans of 1960 which ran in the *Master Cutler*, *Queen of Scots*, *Tees-Tyne Pullman* and *Yorkshire Pullman* and more recently in the charter fleet. At the other end of the scale, the first post-war decade saw the production by Metro-Cammell of 16,500 BR 16-ton mineral wagons.

From January 1961 Metro-Cammell was organised into 4 separate divisions: Railway, Bus, Commercial Vehicle and Engineering Products, both the latter newly formed. The Commercial Vehicle division was set up to deal with the design and manufacture of body work for road vehicles, including covered vans of integral lightweight construction, steel or alloy tipping bodies, tankers in mild steel, stainless or alloy, refrigerated vehicles, bodies for ambulances and fire fighting vehicles and special purpose vehicles (including a prototype taxicab) in fibreglass, then being extensively used in the company's bus bodies. The Engineering Products division was

really a continuation of existing facilities at Saltley and Old Park, such as fabrication, steel stress relieving and heat treatment, sheet metal work, hot and cold press work and drop stamping. Other products included mobile cranes, side loaders and mechanical handling plant, all for outside contract.

The latter two divisions utilised spare capacity brought about by falling orders for buses and, in particular, railway rolling stock for, in general, railway equipment orders open to British manufacturers were shrinking fast from about 1960 onwards as new capacity for rolling-stock building was being created rapidly in the Third World and in Eastern Bloc countries. Political pressure led to indigenous manufacture of railway equipment, and excess production capacity was added to a world industry already suffering from over-supply.

The completion of British Railways' modernisation scheme, and BR's intention to concentrate future work at its own workshops, meant that one of the Metro-Cammell plants would have to close, and the choice eventually fell on Saltley. Although Saltley works was much the older, dating back to 1845, there was a genuine reluctance to see it close. The auctioneer's catalogue, issued in July 1962, correctly described it as the birthplace of the world-renowned railway rolling-stock trade in the City of Birmingham.

LONDON TRANSPORT EXECUTIVE
R59 SURFACE STOCK
NON-DRIVING MOTOR CAR, TYPE 5
CONTRACT NO. RMS.46002

Length over Body End Panels	51' 1.1/4"	Centres of Bogies	35' 0"
Width over Body Panels	8' 11.1/4"	Bogie Wheelbase	7' 10"
Overall Height from Rail	11' 9.5/8"	Hoffmann Roller Type Axleboxes	
Diameter of Wheels on Tread	3' 0"	Seating Accommodation	40
Tare Weight 28 Tons.		4 Cmts. 2 Qrs. (including Motors)	

Built by 2 Qrs. (including Motors)
METROPOLITAN-CAMMELL CARRIAGE AND WAGON CO. LTD.,
ENGLAND
1959

BO.19314   NEG. NO. 9057

Non driving motor car. One of 13 such vehicles ordered by London Transport in 1957 for use on the District Line. Designated R59 surface stock, the aluminium body is shown to good effect as are the bogies and electric current collectors in the up position. *Author's collection*

70

BRITISH TRANSPORT COMMISSION
SECOND CLASS SLEEPING CAR
LOT NO. 30491

Length over Body	64' 6"	Centres of Bogies	46' 6"
Length over Side Buffers	67' 1"	Bogie Wheelbase	8' 6"
Width over Body Panel	9' 0"	Size of Journals	10" x 5"

Tare Weight 40 Tons
Built by
METROPOLITAN-CAMMELL CARRIAGE & WAGON CO. LTD.,
ENGLAND
1959

HO.19015   NEG. NO. 9071.

Above: In July 1957 British Railways ordered 69 1st and 2nd class sleeping cars for their overnight regional sleeper services. The one pictured, built in 1959 – lot no. 30491 – carries its BR no.W2577, allocated to the Western Region.
Author's collection

Below: 1st class Pullman Parlour car 'Emerald', one of the 44 East Coast Pullmans built by Metro-Cammell in 1960/61. Note the Commonwealth bogies.
T.P. Bye

THE PULLMAN CAR COMPANY LIMITED
LOT NO. 3281
1ST CLASS PARLOUR CAR, TYPE D
WITH COMMONWEALTH BOGIES
4' 8.1/2" Gauge

Length over Vestibule Body Ends	64' 6"	Width over Body Panel	9' 3"
Length over Buffers	67' 1"	Centre of Bogies	46' 6"
Height to Top of Roof	12' 4.1/2"	Bogie Wheelbase	8' 6"
Seating Capacity	24	Timken Axleboxes	

Tare Weight 37 Tons 15 Cwts 0 Qrs
Built by
METROPOLITAN-CAMMELL CARRIAGE & WAGON COMPANY LIMITED
ENGLAND
1961

Above: Former Metropolitan Railway Metro-Vick Bo-Bo No.3 *Sir Ralph Verney* heads a train of Metropolitan coaches through Neasden with a Liverpool Street-Chesham train on 9th August 1961.   *J. Edgington*

Below: One of three Western Region 8-car 'Blue Pullman' units built by Metro-Cammell traverses the up main line at Hatherley, Cheltenham in 1960. This was not a regular working, but the signalman at Hatherley box, being 'in the know', was able to photograph this rare event.   *R.Stanton*

The steam era is still much in evidence at Carstairs on 21 June 1965 as 2-car set Sc51227 and 56385 leave the station on the 12.25pm service to Lanark. In 1999 when first generation DMUs had largely disappeared from the railway scene, ScotRail still operated ten Metro-Cammell DMU sets, now designated Class 101, in the Strathclyde area, and some were expected to last into the year 2000. A few more Metro-Cammell sets were also operating on the Hope Valley line between Manchester Piccadilly and Sheffield.

D Percival

Above: South African Railways order for 35 electric locos, on the production line at Old Park, Wednesbury in 1960.

Below: The completed South African Railways type 5.E.1 electric loco 3' 6" gauge.

J. Watkins

SOUTH AFRICAN RAILWAYS
TYPE 5.E.1. ELECTRIC LOCOMOTIVE
3'- 6" GAUGE
Built by
METROPOLITAN-CAMMELL CARRIAGE & WAGON CO.LTD.
BIRMINGHAM, ENGLAND.
(Main Contractors - AEI LTD.)
1960   Neg.No.D.Z.236.

Above: British Transport Commission 30 ton bogie bolster wagon with cast steel bogies, in 1961.   *Author's collection*

Below: 2nd class, Rolls-Royce engined diesel railcar. One of twenty delivered to the Jamaica Railway Corporation during 1962/3. The raised portion of the roof housed the engine radiator and header tank, air ducts, exhaust stack and a water tank for the lavatory.
                                                                                         Author's collection

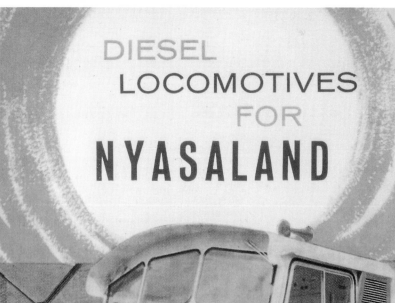

DIESEL
LOCOMOTIVES
FOR
NYASALAND

MECHANICAL PARTS
DESIGNED & BUILT BY

METRO~CAMMELL

MAIN CONTRACTORS
AND SUPPLIERS OF
ELECTRICAL EQUIPMENT

AEI

ENGINES BY
SULZER
BROS. (LONDON) LTD.

METROPOLITAN - CAMMELL CARRIAGE & WAGON CO. LTD

CHAPTER 9

Metro-Cammell
1963-1995 and beyond...

1963 opened with news of another works closure, not one of Metro-Cammell's though, but that of its nearby rival and competitor, the Birmingham Railway Carriage & Wagon Co (BRCW) of Smethwick. Its closure was a reflection of the state of the rolling stock industry as already mentioned at the end of the previous chapter. Metro-Cammell, however, was still fulfilling its underground orders which reached a peak, at the end of 1964, of 1039 tube cars from a continous 5 year production line, but with the depletion of manpower after the closure of Saltley works, the average weekly output (of all types of rolling stock) had fallen from a high of 178 in 1953 to only 19 by the end of 1965.

From 1 January 1965, Metropolitan-Cammell Carriage & Wagon Co Ltd shortened its name to Metropolitan-Cammell Ltd, and a year later became Metropolitan-Cammell (Holdings) Ltd; also taking over the manufacturing interests of Cravens Railway Carriage & Wagon Co of Sheffield. A new subsidiary company, Metro-Cammell Ltd, was formed to take charge of rolling stock production.

The further need to centralise operations on one site was one reason behind the decision, in 1964, to phase out the Old Park works at Wednesbury, which finally closed by the end of 1965. This was followed by the closure of the offices at 1 Metropolitan Road, Saltley, which had survived the shutdown of the adjacent factory in 1962. From 1967 the group's administration was concentrated at 48 Leigh Road, Washwood Heath, the former Midland offices. With this move, 115 years accumulation of drawings and photographs were transferred to the care of Birmingham Central Reference Library where they have been microfilmed and catalogued.

Metro-Cammell secured orders in 1967 to build London Transport's automatic tube trains for its new Victoria line, which, when opened in 1968, was the first complete tube line to be built for 60 years. Apart from the innovation of automatic control, the trains had several visual (new look) features, such as larger side windows double glazed for noise reduction, and driving cabs with wrap-around windscreens giving better visibility. The polished 'silver look' aluminium bodies also added to the appearance of these first modern underground trains. Over the years more and more London Transport cars would be made with aluminium, in fact, in the 1978 (D78) District line stock, only the head stocks and bolsters were of steel, the rest of the underframe and all the body was aluminium except for the maple floor.

Nyasaland Railways took delivery of 8 of these 3' 6" gauge 1200H.P. diesel electric locomotives in 1963. AEI Traction Ltd was the main contractor while Metro-Cammell sub-contracted the mechanical parts. *Metro-Cammell*

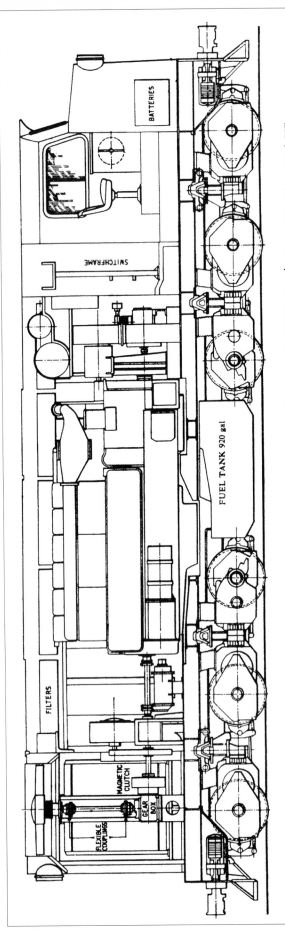

EQUIPMENT IN 1200 H.P. DIESEL-ELECTRIC LOCOMOTIVE FOR TRANS-ZAMBESIA/MALAWI RAILWAYS

Contract in 1966 for 7 - 1,200 H.P. Co-Co Diesel Electric Locomotives for T.Z.R., and 5 for Malawi Railways. Main Contractor, A.E.I. Traction Ltd. Metro-Cammell, sub-contractor for mechanical parts. These were identical to the diesels built in 1963 for Nyasaland.

Gauge	3ft. 6in.	1,067 mm
Weight	81 tons	82,300 kg
Wheel arrangement	Co-Co	
Maximum axle load	13 1/2 tons	13,717 kg
Maximum service speed	50 m.p.h.	80.5 k.p.h.
Engine horsepower	1,200 b.h.p.	
Tractive effort continuous at 8 m.p.h.	40,000 lbs	18,144 kg
Tractive effort maximum	55,000 lbs	24,948 kg
Length over headstocks	43ft. 1. in	13,132 mm
Overall height	13ft. 2. in	4,013 mm
Overall width	9ft. 6. in	2,896 mm
Bogie centres	29ft. 3. in	8,915 mm
Bogie wheelbase	12ft. 0. in	3,658 mm
Wheel diameter	3ft. 0 1/2. in	927 mm
Engine	Sulzer, 6 LDA 28 B-6 cylinder diesel engine, charged at 12 lbs./sq. in. (o.844 kg/sq.cm.) to give an output of 1,200 b.h.p. at 750 r.p.m. under site conditions.	
Cylinder bore	280 mm.	

Above: 1963 4-wheeled aluminium cement wagon for the Portland Cement Company.   *Metro-Cammell*

Below: 1964 L.P.G. tank wagon for ALGECO (UK) Ltd. Note the lifting lugs on the framing.   *Metro-Cammell*

In 1964 Metro-Cammell received an order from Mexican National Railways for 40 Rolls-Royce powered diesel hydraulic railcars. With a top speed of 75mph and only 1st and luxury class accommodation, they were put to work on fast inter city services for Mexico's middle management and executives. This 1966 picture shows 2 first class sets on pre-delivery trials at Stone station in Staffordshire. With an individual overall length of 25.96 metres these railcars were the longest vehicles built by Metro-Cammell.

Metro-Cammell

In 1966 the Pakistan Western Railway placed an order for twenty-nine 3,650hp 5' 6" gauge Bo-Bo electric locomotives, with the 'British Rail Traction Group', a consortium of leading locomotive builders. Metro-Cammell involvement was as main sub-contractor for all mechanical parts. The 80 ton locomotives were 50ft long, 10' 4" wide, and had a tractive effort of 56,000lbs.

Metro-Cammell

Above: The last of twenty-nine 3650hp electric locomotives supplied by English Electric-AEI Traction Ltd. for the Pakistan Western Railway is seen here on the floating crane 'Samson', before being loaded on to the 10,000 ton M.V. Rupta at Birkenhead docks. These locos were part of a £7.5 million 25kV a.c. electrification contract placed by the railway with the British Consortium of Electrification of Pakistan Railways. *English Electric-AEI Traction Ltd.*

Below: A bogie ballast hopper wagon for the 5' 6" gauge Pakistan Western Railways in 1966. *Metro-Cammell*

This publicity photograph depicts mock-ups of various vehicles which helped secure major rapid transit contracts in the late 1970s. From left to right the cars are: Hong Kong; Tyne & Wear; London Transport; Glasgow Underground.
Metro-Cammell

London Transport battery ballast car No.L62, one of a new fleet of vehicles supplied in the early 1980s for permanent way and engineering trains.
Metro-Cammell

Above: D78 surface stock nearing completion in 1979 for London Transport's District Line. These were part of an order for 450 cars replacing older L.T. Stock.

Metro-Cammell

Below: Glasgow Underground opened in 1896. Initially using cars built by the Oldbury Carriage & Wagon Company, the system was cable hauled until electrified in 1935. In 1977 it closed for rebuilding and re-opened in 1980 with new stock seen here outside their depot in Glasgow. Note the 4ft gauge track.

Metro-Cammell

Other orders being completed by Metro-Cammell towards the end of the 1960s included diesel railcars for Mexico, locomotive hauled coaches for the Congo, Rhodesia, electric locomotives for Pakistan, diesel electric locomotives for Malawi, Nigeria and the Trans-Zambesi railways. On the freight side there were 100 ton tanker wagons, some for Shell-Mex & BP Ltd, and containers, the latter built under a recently formed division, Metro-Cammell Containers Ltd. Metro-Cammell-Weymann and engineering products, Metro-Cammell Engineers Ltd, still carried on but the commercial vehicle side had been disbanded.

In 1969 Metro's parent company, Cammell-Laird (Metro) Ltd, underwent a change when Vickers Ltd sold its half share in Metropolitan-Cammell to its partner, Cammell-Laird which renamed itself the Laird Group on 25 September 1970. Metro-Cammell Ltd and its three divisions, now all centred at Washwood Heath, then became wholly owned susidiaries of the Laird Group. This change had little immediate effect on Metro-Cammell, but another, already in the pipeline, would play a part in Metro-Cammell's long term strategy.

As a result of the Government's Transport Act of 1968, British Rail workshops were given powers to tender for, and manufacture, rolling stock for outside contract. Consequently British Rail Engineering Ltd (BREL) was set up in January 1970, principally to still carry its own construction and repair facilities but also to expand into the home and export business. Metro-Cammell's response, perhaps fearing protracted battles for contracts, especially in an ever decreasing export market, was, if you can't beat 'em, join 'em, and as a result, BRE-Metro Ltd was launched early in 1972. Using Metro-Cammell's expertise BREL's workshops would now concentrate on

locomotive and wagon building, as well as coaches, constructing some of the latter, to a basic BR design, for Northern Ireland and the Irish Republic's Coras Iompair Eireann. Metro-Cammell's future now lay in the specialist field in which it had many years experience – passenger coaches and rapid transit stock.

Consequently Metro-Cammell set up a project team, Rapid Transit Limited, able to advise public authorities on complete schemes for heavy and light railways. This was one factor when the first of the new rapid transit contracts was obtained in 1974, for 90 articulated cars (Supertrams) for the Tyne & Wear Metro. This was against competition from Germany and Sweden and other key roles were Metro-Cammell's foresight in building a full size mock up at its own expense and the ability to put together a financial package, with 56 of the Tyne & Wear cars leased from a finance house for 15 years. 1977 saw contracts for a brand new fleet (33 cars) for the 1219mm (4ft) gauge Glasgow Underground. Most rolling-stock is meant to last for 30 to 40 years, but the Glasgow Subway was clearly an exception. In 1976 it was still running its original wooden cars built at Oldbury in 1896. Reconstruction of the line had just begun in 1977 when the Subway was obliged to shut down when cracks appeared in the tunnel roof, and it then remained closed until reopened with new small-profile Metro-Cammell trains in 1980. The most spectacular success in 1977 was winning the rolling-stock contracts for the Hong Kong Mass Transit Railway and Kowloon-Canton suburban line. The contracts were obtained against strong Japanese competition and again a key factor was building a full size mock up. Initially, complete manufacture of the cars was undertaken at the Washwood Heath plant but from 1985 assembly was transferred to Hong Kong using kits of parts

A train on the Hong Kong Mass Transit Railway.

Metro-Cammell

shipped out from the UK and with local labour under the supervision of Metro-Cammell engineers. Over the years, with traffic build up and extensions, repeat orders for both systems has now topped over 1,000 vehicles , 759 on the Hong Kong Mass Railway, which carries 2.5 million passengers daily, and 354 on the Kowloon-Canton Railway, a route carrying over 170 million passengers each year, far greater than many mass transit railways.

The Hong Kong orders compensated for a predicted fall-off in London orders, as London Transport completed its postwar fleet renewal (4,400 cars) and took delivery of 15 Jubilee Line trains, with no further requirements until after 1990. There was a disappointment when a rolling-stock order for Singapore went at an unrealistic price to a Japanese builder apparently trying to stave off closure.

Despite all this activity during 1978-83, in 1984-6 the railway side at Washwood Heath was almost empty, until recovery began in 1987. During the intervening period Metro-Cammell had taken part (with others) in an interesting development, building the Maglev vehicles for Birmingham Airport's shuttle link.

Rolling stock building is a difficult business in which to survive, due to the stop-go cycle in public funding and the unpredictable ordering pattern. Time and again, once-successful firms had been forced to close when a run of good years had been followed by a few bad ones; examples can be quoted from France, Germany and Italy. Just such a gap appeared in Metro-Cammell's order book in 1984. The solution adopted was to change roles from vehicle builder to main contractor, buying in bodyshells and bogies, and concentrating the Metro-Cammell know-how on design, assembly and fitting-out, and some bodyshell suppliers included Procor of Horbury, near Wakefield, and a GEC-Alsthom factory near Barcelona, Spain.

Replacement of British Rail's life expired diesel railcar fleet, for which both the PTEs and trade unions had long been pressing, began in 1987 with a Metro-Cammell contract for 114 two-car trains of Class 156, though Metro's own short range design (BR Class 151) was not adopted. Another design not adopted was for a new generation of tube trains despite Metro-Cammell's long association with London Transport. Three prototypes were trialled in 1987, two built by Metro-Cammell the other by BREL, after which, in an ironic twist, Metro's former 1970s partner secured the order for the Central Line's 1992 stock.

1989 saw the first deliveries of 283 Mark 4 locomotive hauled

Class 156 D.M.U. 'Sprinter' No.156402 comprising vehicles No.52402/57402 in provisional sector livery. Introduced in 1987, they had two Cummins engines rated at 285hp.

Metro-Cammell

coaches and driving van trailers for the newly electrified East Coast main line, some fitting out of the coach interiors being done by sub-contractors. These contract partnerships had already crossed national boundaries, especially the EC countries where rail vehicle suppliers had not only been allowed to tender but formed international alliances, and as a result, in a logical move Metro-Cammell joined the Anglo-French group GEC-Alsthom. In 1992 the Washwood Heath plant under its new name, GEC-Alsthom Metro-Cammell secured contracts for the supply of Class 465 and 466 Networker electrical multiple units for the former Southern Region London suburban lines and it was also chosen to assemble some of the 38 prestigious Eurostar high speed trains. The first of 15, international, Eurostar trains, each about 400 metres long, assembled and fully tested in Birmingham, arrived in France at the end of October 1993. These were followed by four shorter Eurostar trains intended for UK regional services north of London, and 139 coaches for the Nightstar services. However at the time of writing the fate of these regional trains and coaches built for the aborted Nightstar services await the outcome of financial talks.

After a few years gap contracts were received in the mid 1990s from London Underground for 354 cars for the Jubilee Line extension (1996 stock) and 636 cars for the upgraded Northern Line, whilst a special overseas order completed in 1998 was for seven new generation, 4-car EMU train sets for the Arlanda Airport Railway, a 40 km long rail shuttle link between Stockholm and the airport. Contracts have also been obtained from various privatised rail companies in the UK and work in progress or on order during 1999 included 'Juniper' EMUs for the Gatwick Express service; class 175 'Coradia' DMUs for First North Western (which had some test runs on the Severn Valley Railway); and class 180 DMUs for First Great Western.

As we enter the twenty-first century the first of the UK's new generation, futuristic look trains have been delivered whilst the corporate image of the Washwood Heath plant has also changed with yet another name change to Alstom Transport Limited. The news that Alstom, in conjunction with Fiat, is to build the Virgin Group's Tilting EMUs at Washwood Heath appears to bode well for the immediate future.

The first of these tilting trains is due to go into service on the West Coast main line in March 2001 and delivery of all 54 sets is due to be completed by May 2002. What better way could be found of marking over 150 years of craftmanship by Joseph Wright and his successors.

Class 460 'Juniper' electric multiple units being built for the Gatwick Express in October 1998.   *Metro-Cammell*

CHAPTER 10

Buses and Trolleybuses
A Brief History

Although the train had long since replaced the mail coach, Metropolitan Amalgamated still had a sideline in horse-drawn road vehicles until at least 1906, mainly drays and carriers' carts. It re-entered the road passenger vehicle market in 1929, and stayed in it for sixty years.

The fall in demand for rail vehicles in 1928/29 pointed to a need for diversification, and a decision was taken to apply Metropolitan's experience with steel railway vehicles to the construction of steel-framed bus bodies. Metal framed bodywork was rare, most vehicles then (and for many years afterwards) being of composite construction, with timber frames and metal panels. About 200 metal bus bodies had been made elsewhere since 1925, mostly using rolled sections in non-ferrous alloys. Another variation was that used by Weymann of Addlestone, Surrey, whose motor car and coach bodies had a metal-jointed wooden frame covered with leathercloth. While appropriate for Bentley and other cars, this was not so suitable for larger vehicles, and Weymann had turned to metal panelling, for example in the first London Green Line coaches.

Metropolitan-Cammell's engineers designed and patented in 1929 the main features of their proposed steel-framed bus body, and in July 1932 formed an alliance with Weymann's Motor Bodies (1925) Ltd, to form a joint sales company, Metropolitan-Cammell-Weymann Motor Bodies Ltd (MCW) to handle and expand both companies' products. Metropolitan's first steel-framed bus bodies were bought by Birmingham Corporation in 1930, and about 7000 MCW bodies were produced in the next seven years at Addlestone and Washwood Heath. Controversy was rife throughout the industry as to the rival merits of all-metal and composite bodywork, the protagonists of metal bodywork sometimes using gruesome photographs of accident-damaged vehicles to show that metal bodies gave greater protection. One of the 1930 prototypes was tested by having a railway truck shunted into it, to show the strength of the body and the localisation of the damage. On another occasion a steam lorry was run into the back of a bus during a transport managers' visit and the damage was repaired while the visitors were walking round the works.

One of the most revolutionary buses of the 1930s was the side engined AEC Q series introduced in 1932. The side engine was a radical departure from the traditional engine in front and it allowed body builders to come up with some very advanced looking bodies. Most of the Q were single deck with bodies by various builders including Metro-Cammell but a few double

Birmingham City Transport was obviously a regular buyer of Metro-Cammell vehicles with the factories situated within the city. Represented here at Bridgnorth on the Severn Valley Railway are former BCT No.1107 (CVP207) one of the numerous Daimler COG 5 buses with Metro-Cammell bodies delivered between1934-1939, alongside 1486 (GOE486) another Metro-Cammell example on a Daimler CVA6 chassis dating from 1947. Taken on 3 August 1974 both vehicles are currently in preservation, 1107 with the1685 Group, and 1486 with Mr. C. Hawketts.   *Garry Yates*

Above: Perhaps the most famous class of buses ever built were the London Transport A.E.C. RT class with 4825 examples being built between 1939 and 1959. Many of the class had Park Royal bodies, with Metro-Cammell/Weymann building hundreds although externally there was little difference. The final day of RT operation was on 7 April 1979 when RT624 (now preserved at the Midland Bus Museum), entered Barking depot for the final time. Seen some six years earlier on 9 September 1973 at Bromley depot is RT2272 (KGU301) one of a Weymann bodied batch of buses. Alongside is RT4583 (NLP576), a Park Royal bodied example. *Garry Yates*

Below: Birmingham was well known for its 'Tin Front' buses represented here by 2908 (JOJ908) a 1952 built Metro-Cammell bodied Guy Arab IV. Wearing the early West Midlands PTE colour scheme it was photographed in the Handsworth area of Birmingham on the famous Outer-Circle route on 15 August1974. Three years later in 1977 saw the end of the 'Tin Fronts' when the last vehicles were withdrawn some having been in service for 25 years! *Garry Yates*

deck versions were also built, some with attractive Metro-Cammell bodies with wide front entrances ahead of the set back front axle. Although ahead of its time the Q was only a relative success, but some of the body features would reappear years later in other designs in which Metro-Cammell became involved. MCW all-metal bus bodies earned themselves a generally good reputation, often giving trouble-free service for twice the life anticipated when they were built. Municipal customers included Birmingham, Coventry, Leicester, Manchester, Nottingham, Salford and Wallasey: others included British Electric Traction group customers such as Midland Red and Rhondda. Trolleybus bodies built by MCW included batches for Birmingham, Derby, Newcastle and London, many of the 1937-39 London vehicles remaining in service until 1960-62. Relatively few single-deckers were built, perhaps because the smaller operators preferred timber-framed bodies for ease of in-house repair.

MCW built up a useful export trade in bus and trolleybus bodies, the latter especially to South Africa. Forty-three trolleybuses awaiting shipment to Durban and Johannesburg were diverted to London during the War, replacements being built afterwards. The successful use of these 8ft wide vehicles in wartime London (and others in Bradford and Birmingham) played a key role in the postwar relaxation in the UK rules on vehicle width. This trade formed the basis in 1946 for the formation of a local MCW subsidiary, Bus Bodies (SA) Ltd of Port Elizabeth, whose British-style 'Busaf' vehicles are a familiar sight in South Africa, along with locally assembled Land Rovers with bodies built in Port Elizabeth. Other Metro-Cammell

subsidiaries were set up in India (Southern Structurals Ltd, Madras) and Rhodesia (Zambesi Coach Works, Salisbury), the latter in 1957 jointly with Leyland.

During the 1939-45 War the Birmingham factories switched to making military vehicles, though Addlestone produced 'utility' bodywork for 687 buses and 35 trolleybuses in 1942-45. MCW took over the wartime Sterling bomber factory at Elmdon, Birmingham and reopened it in 1946 as a bus works. By 1950 MCW could claim to have built 12,000 all-metal bus bodies at Elmdon, Addlestone and Washwood Heath, over 1700 of them for Birmingham Corporation and a similar number for London Transport; by 1953 the total had reached 16,000, many being for export. 1950 saw the launch of MCW's best-selling export, the single-deck 'Olympic' (jointly with Leyland) which sold particularly well in South America.

Metal construction was now the industry standard, due partly to wartime experience in aircraft construction, but also to the postwar shortage of seasoned timber and the ready availability of body components from Metal Sections Ltd, of Oldbury.

Post-war economies by bus operators prompted a call for lighter buses and in 1952 Daimler came up with a double deck bus weighing only 6 1/2 tons. The body was a new design by Metro-Cammell, the 'Orion', weighing just under two tons but at the expense of comfort for passengers, lacking, as it was, interior panel lining and insulation. Despite derogatory remarks from some operators and the general public, the 'Orion', on various chassis, went on to give nearly twenty years service.

Body fronts were changing too, the early 1950s bringing in

Photographed in Edinburgh's famous Princess Street is Edinburgh Corporation No.444 (LFS444), one of a large batch of Leyland Titan PD2/20s bodied by Metro-Cammell between 1954-6. (401-600). These were followed by a further batch (701-800) in 1956-7. Displaying Edinburgh Corporation's virtually unchanged fleet livery the photograph was taken on 22 August 1974, and needless to say these days the registration would be worth a small fortune!   *Garry Yates*

Left: Bournemouth had a large trolleybus system until its' demise in the mid-sixties. In fact the depot where this picture was taken was probably the most modern trolley-bus depot in the country, having been built in the late 1950s. 297 (297LJ) pictured here represents the final batch of Weymann bodied trolleybuses delivered to the Corporation between 1958-61. Bournemouth always preferred dual-door buses and these were no exception. Seen on 1 September 1973 the bus, which is now in preservation, was about to leave (under tow!) on the Bournemouth/Bath run.

Garry Yates

the 'wide look', the so-called tin front double deckers, although the drivers still sat in isolation in a seperate cab. However a more drastic change was to come with Metro-Cammell playing a major part in what probably did more than any other to influence the future shape of double deck buses in this country and abroad, and that was the launch of the Leyland 'Atlantean' in 1956. The 'Atlantean' had its engine mounted transversely at the rear, and had a set back front axle allowing an entrance door to be fitted ahead of it, as in the 1930s AEC Q. The flat underframe had an integrally mounted 78 seat Metro-Cammell body, but from 1958 production models had a separate Leyland chassis and a Metro-Cammell body with the rear engine enclosed in a 'boot'.

Initial sales were slow but by the time they had picked up in the late 1960s many other body builders were competing against Metro-Cammell with more exciting body styles, however Metro-Cammell continued to build batches until 1980. The last 'Atlantean' was delivered in 1984, by which time over 15000 had been built, many for export, to such diverse countries as Australia , Ecuador, India, Kuwait, Philippines and Uruguay to name a few, but all emanating from Metro-Cammell's original 1956 design.

In 1963 Weymanns were bought out but the falling demand for buses as car ownership rose in the early 1960s was one reason which brought about the closure of Addlestone in 1965, the factory and contents being sold by auction in March 1966. The sales company Metropolitan-Cammell-Weymann Ltd then became the subsidiary responsible for bus production.

Trolleybus production had resumed briefly in 1948 with some handsome three-axle vehicles for Glasgow, London and Newcastle, of which the London examples were later sold to Spain. Postwar MCW trolleybus exports included batches for Johannesburg and Auckland. A South African enquiry in 1980 caused a new trolleybus to be designed, but it never left the drawing-board. In 1970, when space became available at Washwood Heath, bus production was moved back from Elmdon which closed, so concentrating all Metro-Cammell activity on one site.

Until the early 1970s MCW was only a body builder. The customer chose and bought the chassis, at that time usually from Leyland. Leyland's government-backed plan for an integral bus factory at Workington seemed likely to divert much trade away from MCW; its response was a joint venture with Scania

of Sweden, fitting MCW bodies to Scania chassis as the single-deck 'Metro-Scania' and the double-deck 'Metropolitan'. When this partnership was dissolved a few years later, MCW went solo with the 'Metrobus', an aluminium-bodied air-sprung rear-engined integral double-decker, assembled at Washwood Heath with bought-in Rockwell main chassis members, Kirkstall axles, a choice of Gardner or Rolls-Royce engine, and a Voith gearbox. Production began in 1977, and within two years MCW's share of the UK double-deck market had risen from 20% to 60%. The largest customers (out of 28) were London Transport and West Midlands PTE, and the biggest buses were 60 3-axle 'Metrobuses' for China Motor Bus Co of Hong Kong, each with a legal capacity of 148, but often exceeded. The same period saw the successful launch of the 'Metrocab' taxi.

The early 1980s saw many continental built double deck coaches on Britain's motorways, and to meet a demand for home produced models several bus builders came up with some interesting vehicles, Metro-Cammell's response being the 'Metroliner' in 1983. Based on a Hong Kong Metro bus chassis, the 'Metroliner' was a 12 metre long, 3 axle double deck coach with a rear mounted Cummins engine. Internally it was fitted out with soft trim, reclining seats, double glazing and optional video screens. Several operators took delivery including the National Bus Company, some coaches running under the National Express logo. Metro-Cammell's entry into the coach business was very brief for market share is unfortunately not the same as market size and the first cloud on the horizon was the phased ending of the Government's bus grant (by 1984), causing operators to keep buses in service longer, typically 15 to 18 years instead of 10 to 14. Then there was the mini-bus revolution, with small buses on close headways, often displacing double-deckers; MCW responded by introducing its own purpose-built midibus, the 'Metrorider'. The greater headache was deregulation, these three factors combining to cause the UK double-deck market to shrink from 2,000 buses per year in 1980 to a mere 300 ten years later. In 1950, MCW's three factories alone were building 2,000 buses per year. Coinciding as it did with a quiet period on the rail side, MCW had to cut its losses, and 'Metrobus' production ceased in 1989, the taxi and midibus operations being sold to other manufacturers. The former bus works at Leigh Road is still in use, but as reception and storage areas for rail vehicle body-shells and components.

Above: Metro-Cammell's answer to 'complete' bus builders (such as Leyland) was to introduce its own designed and built Metrobus in 1977. Initially powered by a 170bhp Gardner engine following trials with West Midlands PTE, London Transport and Chinabus, some were fitted with an alternative 180bhp Rolls Royce Eagle unit. Pictured is one of the pre-production single door Metrobus operated by West Midlands PTE. Other operators such as London Transport favoured the 2-door, centre exit type.

Metro-Cammell

Below: Pre-production 2-door, centre exit, Metrobus carrying the colours of London Transport, but with a Birmingham registration plate.

Metro-Cammell

Above: In the late 1970s Metro-Cammell designed and built the Metrobus in competition with the Leyland Titan. This bus was very successful with large orders from London Transport (1480 built); West Midlands PTE (1124 built) and many other operators bought them in smaller numbers. The Titan due to its higher cost, never really took off except in London so the threatened competition never materialised. The Mark 1 Metrobus was replaced by the Mark 2 in 1982 with a completely restyled body and building continued more or less until the end of Metro-Cammell with the final examples going to West Midlands PTE and Greater Glasgow PTE in 1990. Northern General had a small batch of Mark 1 Metrobuses and pictured here on 22 August 1981 is No.3493 (DVK493W) in Newcastle-Upon-Tyne city centre displaying the famous 'Shop at Binns' advert, at one time, found on most buses in the North East. *Garry Yates*

Below: Metro-Cammell never really built coach bodies although a small number of 'Metroliner' coaches were built in the 1980s mainly going to East Kent. Weymann however built coaches for various operators throughout the years. Sheffield Corporation had several small batches of Weymann bodied coaches and pictured here at Burton-on-Trent bus station, on 8 May 1976 operating for Stevensons, is former Sheffield Omnibus No.1314 (1914WA), a 1961 built Weymann Fanfare Coach. Stevensons of Uttoxeter was well known for its variety of second hand vehicles until it was finally absorbed into the Midland Red North fleet, now part of the Arriva empire. *Garry Yates*

CHAPTER 11

Metro-Cammell Family Tree

METROPOLITAN RAILWAY CARRIAGE & WAGON COMPANY LTD, SALTLEY, BIRMINGHAM.
(SUCCESSORS OF JOSEPH WRIGHT & SONS.)
The company was formed in 1862 as successors of Joseph Wright & Sons and continued to develop steadily until by 1896 it had outgrown its original Memorandum of Association and a new company bearing the same name was formed to take over the greatly extended business.

Six years later in 1902 the first step in the rationalisation of the rolling stock industry was made when the Metropolitan Amalgamated Railway Carriage & Wagon Company Ltd was formed with a share capital of £1,500,000 to take over the business of the Metropolitan Company and amalgamate it with the following well known rolling stock companies:
The Ashbury Railway Carriage & Iron Company Ltd
Brown Marshalls & Company
The Lancaster Railway Carriage & Wagon Company Ltd
The Oldbury Railway Carriage & Wagon Company Ltd

The object of the almagamation was to centralise the rolling stock companies and to focus in one great concern the skill and experience of these firms. In order that this might be achieved the personnel and businesses of the absorbed rolling stock companies were gradually transferred to Saltley and the factories closed down. In the same year, in order that they might have their own source of supplies for building rolling stock, the Amalgamated Company acquired the whole of the assets and undertaking of the Patent Shaft & Axletree Company Ltd of Wednesbury, an important firm of iron and steel manufacturers having their own rolling mills and producing plates, bars, sections, switches and crossings, wheels, axles etc and having a high reputation as bridge builders. From 1905 until 1908 Metropolitan Amalgamated occupied the Hadley Castle Car Works of George F Milnes, the well known tram builder, who had moved from Birkenhead to Hadley in 1900. As well as building trams at Hadley, before the factory closed in 1904, Milnes was credited as having built bodies there for Milnes-Daimler buses used by the GWR on the Helston-Lizard service,which started in 1903.

In 1919 Vickers Ltd acquired the shares of the Metropolitan Company. In the same year Cammell-Laird & Company Ltd of Sheffield and Birkenhead commenced the manufacture of railway rolling stock at the National Ordnance factory in Nottingham, which they had managed during the Great War on behalf of the government and which they shortly afterwards purchased.

The Nottingham works were actively engaged in the production of rolling stock from 1919 to 1931 but owing to the trade depression then prevailing, the business was transferred to Saltley and the works were sold. Concurrently with this new venture Cammell-Laird & Company obtained a controlling interest in the Midland Railway Carriage & Wagon Company Ltd

of Washwood Heath, Birmingham, – one of the foremost rolling stock undertakings in the country, and four years later acquired control of the Leeds Forge Company Ltd of Armley, Leeds, with its railway carriage works at Newlay and its subsidiaries the Newlay Wheel Company Ltd and the Bristol Wagon & Carriage Works Company Ltd. Shortly afterwards in 1927 the Metropolitan Company purchased the business of the Blake Boiler Wagon & Engineering Company Ltd of Darlington and transferred it to Saltley.

In 1929 Vickers Ltd and Cammell-Laird & Company merged their rolling stock interests to form Metropolitan-Cammell Carriage & Wagon Company Ltd with its Head Office at Saltley, the share capital being held by the parent companies in equal proportions. Soon after the formation of the new Metropolitan-Cammell organisation a department was set up to investigate the possibility of extending manufacture beyond railway rolling stock, and the outcome was the decision to embark on the production of 'all metal' omnibus bodies based on an extruded pillar section, for which the company secured a patent. Metro-Cammell thus became the pioneers of the modern all metal omnibus body.

At the outbreak of the Second World War production facilities were diverted to armament production and the company became the largest suppliers of fighting tanks in the country.

In 1965 the company was restyled Metropolitan-Cammell Ltd, and in the following year the manufacturing interests of Craven Railway Carriage & Wagon Company Ltd were absorbed; in 1967 Head Office was transferred to the Midland works at Washwood Heath.

Vickers disposed of their interest in 1969 and in 1970 the company became a wholly owned subsidiary of Cammell-Laird, renamed the Laird Group.

In 1989 Metro-Cammell became part of G E C-Alsthom, since renamed in 1998 Alstom Transport Ltd.

ASHBURY RAILWAY CARRIAGE & IRON COMPANY LIMITED, OPENSHAW & ARDWICK, MANCHESTER.
The Ashbury works at Manchester were founded by a Mr John Ashbury about the middle of the nineteenth century, and the business was converted into a Limited Liability Company in 1862. The Company were builders of rolling stock at Openshaw, Manchester and iron manufacturers at Ardwick, Manchester.
1902: Absorbed into Metropolitan Amalgated Railway Carriage & Wagon Company and business transferred to Saltley.

BROWN MARSHALLS LIMITED.
Early records show that the company's predecessors, Messrs, Brown & Marshalls, were well known manufacturers of stage coaches in small premises at New Canal Street, Birmingham, and afterwards of railway carriages and wagons. In 1853 the firm moved to Adderley Park, Birmingham where they built the Brittania Works well known in the early days of rolling stock

manufacture. In 1867 the business was converted into a Limited Liability Company and continued to produce rolling stock of every description for home and foreign railways, specialising in work of a luxurious character; special mention must be made of the Peninsula and Oriental Express dining cars, completed in 1892 for the Compagnie Internationale des Wagons Lits et des Grands Express Europeans of Paris, which ran between Calais and Brindisi connecting with the Peninsular and Oriental Steamers. The business was transferred to Saltley in 1908 and the works were sold to the Wolseley Tool and Motor Car Company Limited in 1911, the site later being occupied by Morris Commercial Cars Limited.

1902: Absorbed into The Metropolitan Amalgamated Railway Carriage & Wagon Company Ltd.

1908: Business transferred to Saltley.

1911: Works sold to the Wolseley Tool & Motor Company.

LANCASTER RAILWAY CARRIAGE & WAGON COMPANY, LANCASTER.

The Lancaster Company was formed in 1863 and owned extensive works on the outskirts of Lancaster where it produced railway rolling stock of all descriptions, tramcars, wheel & axles, etc; and had a reputation for work of a very high class character. The company's early years were difficult financially, but by the 1880s it employed 800 men and was doing useful business, such as building 140 vehicles for a new metre gauge railway in Brazil. In 1885 it was also constructing tramcars for London, Blackpool and Bury. By 1892 up to 1400 men were employed on a 15-acre site.

1902: Absorbed into Metropolitan Amalgamated Railway Carriage & Wagon Company.

1908: Works closed – business transferred to Saltley.

OLDBURY RAILWAY CARRIAGE & WAGON COMPANY LIMITED, OLDBURY.

This business originated at Bromsgrove, Worcestershire, its founder being a Mr R W Johnson who built a factory about the middle of the last century adjoining Bromsgrove station on the old Midland Railway. Later he transferred his activities to Oldbury, where he built and equipped a new factory which he sold in 1865 to the Railway Carriage Company Limited, which was formed to take over the business. The company was ideally situated adjoining the London & North Western Railway, it had a pit-shaft drawing coal within 5 yards of the workshops and at least 30 iron rolling mills within a 2 mile radius, and a canal connection with Liverpool and London which was used for shipments abroad. In 1886 the Oldbury Railway Carriage & Wagon Company Limited was formed to take over the business of the earlier company. The Oldbury Company was an extremely well managed concern and its reputation in the industry was second to none.

1902: Absorbed into Metropolitan Amalgamated Railway Carriage & Wagon Company.

1932: Works closed.

PATENT SHAFT & AXLETREE COMPANY LTD, WEDNESBURY, STAFFS. (PATENT SHAFT STEEL WORKS).

The Patent Shaft Company had its origins in the early 1830s, following an idea by a local Baptist minister, the Rev. James Hardy, for faggotted cart axles of forged iron built like segments of an orange and forged together under a hammer. This he thought would give much greater strength than axles then being forged with layers of flat or square iron.

Hardy's idea proved a success, so much so, that he took out a patent (No. 6807) on 4 April 1835, and together with a local grocer, who provided the money to buy a small ironworks, went into partnership to make 'Hardys Patent Axletree'.

Although a good product, early manufacturing had little sale until the business was taken over in 1840 by Charles Geach, a Birmingham banker, and Thomas Walker who had been employed as a clerk at Rev. Hardy's works. From there on, the Patent Shaft & Axletree Co, as it then became, started to expand the Brunswick ironworks and in 1844 the LNWR gave the company a boost by adopting the Patent Axle exclusively for use in its rolling stock.

By 1854 the works employed more than 800 men and in 1864, the Patent Shaft Axletree Company Ltd was formed with Thomas Walker as chairman. This was followed in 1867 by the acquisition of the neighbouring company of Messrs Lloyds-Fosters & Co. whose Monway and Old Park works had blast furnaces, Bessemer steel works, rolling mills, railway wheel and axle works, bridge & girder shops and collieries. Lloyd-Fosters had been in business at Wednesbury since 1818 when Samuel Lloyd (a member of the banking family) started mining coal and ironstone in a district of Wednesbury known as Old Park, eventually building a factory there and branching out into the iron and steel trade. Old Park works had in fact supplied the ironwork for London's Blackfriars Bridge, but as a result of the contractor not being able to pay his monthly account, Lloyds-Fosters agreed to defer payment until the contractor was able to which in the event he never did. This eventually incurred Lloyd-Fosters a heavy loss of £250,000 which forced them to sell out to the Patent Shaft Co.

1902: Patent Shaft & Axletree Company Ltd absorbed into Metropolitan Amalgamated Railway Carriage & Wagon Company.

Old Park works railway wagon building facilities integrated with Metropolitan.

Amalgamated around 1919, the other factories concentrating on steel making and rolling etc.

1965: Old Park works phased out and closed.

1980: Patent Shaft Steel Works (1959) Ltd closed by the Laird Group (Metro-Cammell's parent company).

CAMMELL-LAIRD LIMITED

In 1810 William Laird came to Liverpool to seek business for his father's Greenock ropeworks, and acquired land at Birkenhead with the aim of developing port facilities. The scheme fell through and he utilised the land to build a boiler works and housing for his workers and their families. The first order to build a ship was in 1812, and the interests of the firm began to expand with the development of iron ships, and in 1840 came the first order for naval vessels.

In 1903, with the object of forming a group of companies able to see a job right through, from raw materials to finished product, Laird Brothers (as the company was now called) teamed up with Charles Cammell & Company Limited, a large steel producer in Sheffield which had been formed in 1828 by Charles Cammell from whom Lairds Limited obtained armour plate for their naval vessels. The new company, Cammell-Laird Limited, began building railway rolling stock in Nottingham in 1919 and in the same year absorbed the Midland Railway Carriage & Wagon Company.

SPECIFICATION:

Gauge 5' 6"

Swing Bridge .	Clear opening	82' 0"
	Centres of bearings	212' 9"
Carrying Railway	Width, centres of main girders . . .	16' 6"
	Height at centre of main girders . . .	24' 0"
Total weight of bridge		384 tons

This splendid swing bridge, built by the Patent Shaft Co. for the Buenos Aires Great Southern Railway, featured in a Metropolitan Carriage Wagon & Finance Co. pamphlet dated August 1912   *C.J. Walker collection*

The Patent Shaft & Axletree Company, Ltd.
Wednesbury, England

INCORPORATED WITH

The Metropolitan Carriage Wagon & Finance Co., Ltd.
Saltley, Birmingham, England

Manufacturers of BRIDGES, CARRIAGES, WAGONS, WHEELS and AXLES, ROLLED STEEL DISC WHEELS, SWITCHES and CROSSINGS, TURNTABLES, WATER CRANES, TANKS, BOGIES, UNDERFRAMES, ROOFING, ETC., ETC.

London Office . . . 36, Victoria Street, Westminster

MIDLAND RAILWAY CARRIAGE & WAGON COMPANY LIMITED, MIDLAND WORKS, WASHWOOD HEATH, BIRMINGHAM.

Of the companies comprising the Cammell-Laird Group, the Midland Railway Carriage & Wagon Company Limited is the oldest; it was formed in 1853 for the purpose of purchasing railway wagons and letting them out on hire to private owners, but it commenced to build rolling stock itself in 1864, when works were acquired in Landor Street, Saltley, Birmingham. In 1877 the Abbey Works at Shrewsbury were purchased and production at both works continued on an ever increasing scale. In 1907 the company purchased a freehold site of some 51 acres at Washwood Heath, Birmingham, for the erection of a new works to cope with a demand for rolling stock of a heavier type than that for which its existing works had been designed. The new works were commenced in 1909 and completed in 1912, and the businesses at Landor Street and Shrewsbury were transferred to new premises which constituted the Midland Works of the Metropolitan-Cammell Company.

1919: Absorbed into Cammell-Laird & Company Limited.
1929: Amalgamated with Metropolitan-Cammell Carriage & Wagon Company Limited.

The Midland works is now home to Metro-Cammell successors, Alstom Transport Limited.

VICKERS LIMITED

Established at Sheffield in 1829 as Naylor Hutchison and Vickers, iron founders and engineers (later Naylor Vickers & Company Limited), the company were pioneers in the engineering of iron ships and the casting of screw propellers for steam powered ships, including naval vessels. In 1897 the company was renamed Vickers Sons & Maxim Limited, having acquired in that year the Maxim Nordenfelt Guns & Ammunition Company and Naval Construction and Armaments Company of Barrow. Further acquisitions in the early 1900s were Loco Limited, Cooke Toughton & Sims, Whitehead Torpedo Company, and the Wolseley Tool & Motor Company was also set up.

The Airship Guarantee Corporation was formed in 1923 to build the R100 and later the ill-fated R101. After acquiring Variable Speed Gear Limited in 1924 a new company, Vickers-Armstrong Limited, was formed and in 1928/9 the rolling stock interests of the company were merged with those of Cammell-Laird to form the jointly owned subsidiary Metropolitan-Cammell Limited. At this time Supermarine Aviation Works Limited was acquired and Vickers (Aviation) Limited formed, and the steel interests of Vickers-Armstrong and Cammell-Laird were joined to form the English Steel Corporation Limited. Numerous acquisitions followed, leading to the establishment of groups embracing:

Computers (International Computers &Tabulators)
British Aircraft Corporation
Printing Machinery Group
Office Equipment Group

Achievements include Britain's first 100,000 ton tanker; the 'Viscount' aircraft; and, in war time, the 'Spitfire'; the 'Wellington' Bomber and the 'Valentine' tank.

LEEDS FORGE COMPANY LIMITED
WORKS AT ARMLEY & NEWLAY, LEEDS,
WITH SUBSIDIARY AT BRISTOL (1920-1924).

The Leeds Forge Company Limited was formed in 1873 to take over the business of toolmakers carried on by Messrs Samson & William Fox, and to erect works for the manufacture of iron and steel. From 1877 onwards the company produced Fox's Corrugated Furnaces which became world famous, and the manufacture of rolling stock of pressed steel construction was commenced in 1887.

The Leeds Forge Company took an active part in the design, development and construction of all-steel carriages whilst their wagons were of a distinctive design with low tare weights; they specialised also in the manufacture of pressed steel carriage and wagon bodies, and underframes.

1923: Absorbed into Cammell-Laird & Co. Ltd
1929: Works closed and business transferred to Saltley.

BRISTOL WAGON & CARRIAGE COMPANY LIMITED, BRISTOL.

The Bristol Wagon & Carriage Company Limited was formed in 1856 to take over a business of agriculture implement and machine makers, wheelwrights and iron founders, and to manufacture rolling stock of all descriptions. The Company was acquired by the Leeds Forge Company Limited in 1920 and the business (with the exception of the motor and agriculture portions, which were separately disposed of) was transferred to Leeds in 1924 and the Company was wound up.

METRO-CAMMELL – WEYMANN (MCW).

Weymanns Motor Bodies (1925) Limited was formed in 1925 at Addlestone, Surrey, to manufacture a new type of motor car and later motor coach bodies consisting of a light and flexible metal-jointed wooden frame covered with leather cloth, which became very popular, but in its final development metal panels replaced the fabric covering. In 1932 Metropolitan-Cammell-Weymann was set up as a joint organisation after the two manufacturing companies had agreed to pool their body-building resources, bus body building having been introduced at Metro-Cammell in 1929. In 1946 MCW took over a wartime aircraft factory at Elmdon in which to build buses. In 1965 the Addlestone factory closed and all production was then concentrated at MCW in Birmingham (Elmdon & Washwood Heath), Elmdon was closed in 1970 and MCW ceased all bus production in 1989.

BRE-METRO LIMITED.

Formed as an export sales company in 1970 to administer jointly the export and sales interests of British Rail Engineering Ltd – the rolling stock manufacturing arm of the British Railways Board – and Metro-Cammell Limited. The object of the company was to exploit the international sales resources and technical experience gained over 130 years by Metro-Cammell, and the large productive capacity and testing facilities of British Rail.

The registered office was at Metro-Cammell but the centre of administration moved in 1972 to offices at 274-280 Bishopsgate, London.

The partnership was disolved in the early 1980s following reorganisation within British Rail. BREL was privatised in 1989 and is now known as ADTRANZ.

Above: The offices of Metro-Cammell's successors, Alsthom Transport Limited in Leigh Road, Washwood Heath, Birmingham. These were the former offices of the Midland Railway-Carriage & Wagon Company which was absorbed into the 'Metro' Group in 1929.   *Metro-Cammell*

Below: An informal gathering of G.E.C-Alsthom staff at Washwood Heath. The two coaches awaiting completion are 'Euro-Star' buffet cars, clearly identified by the large windows.   *Metro-Cammell*

APPENDIX 1

ORDERS PRODUCED BY METROPOLITAN CAMMELL LIMITED FOR MOTOR COACHES, DIESEL AND ELECTRIC LOCOMOTIVES, RAILCARS BETWEEN 1946 AND 1968

DATE OF ORDER	RAILWAY UNDERTAKING	No.	DESCRIPTION
18.7.45	Central Railway of Brazil	30	3 Coach Units (including 30 Motor Coaches)
29.4.47	Egyptian Railways	10	Triple-Articulated Railcare
19.12.47	Indian Railways	56	Electric Motor Coaches
15.12.48	London Transport Board	90	Motor Coaches
22.4.49	South African Railways	17	1st Class Motor Coaches
16.10.50	South African Railways	6	Ist Class Motor Coaches
1.2.51	Nigeria Railways	2	Triple Unit Railcars
23.6.52	South African Railways	10	1st Class Motor Coaches
25.3.54	Central Railway of Brazil	50	3 Car Electric Train Units
		50	Motor Coaches
		100	Trailer Coaches
11.5.54.	Coras Iompair Eireann	60	Diesel Electric Locos 1200hp
		34	Diesel Electric Locos 550hp
May 1954-Jan 1959	British Railways	798	Diesel Railcars in multiple units varying from 1 to 4 car
20.10.54	London Transport Board		Prototype Train, including 5 Motor Cars, 7-car Train
16.6.55	Indian Government Railways	18	Motor Coach Shells, Underframes and Bogies.
1.7.55	South African Railways	105	Motor Coaches
		244	Trailer Coaches
14.12.56	British Railways	5	Train Sets – Diesel Multiple De Luxe Express Service (36 Coaches)
3.12.57	London Transport Board	13	Non-Driving Motor Cars
15.5.58	London Transport Board	76	7 Car Trains including
		304	Driving Motor Cars
		76	Non-Driving Motor Cars
		152	Trailer Cars
21.5.59	Metropolitan-Vickers Electrical Co. Ltd. (for South African Railways)	35	Electric Locos (Type 5E1) 2280hp
28.3.60	London Transport Board	57	Non-Driving Motor Cars
27.10.60	Jamaica Railways	17	Diesel Railcars
7.4.61	London Transport Board	169	Driving Motor Cars Type A
		169	Driving Motor Cars Type D
		169	Non-Driving Motor Cars
15.3.61	Jamaica Railways	3	Diesel Railcars
14.3.62	Nyasaland Railways	8	D.E. Locos 1200hp
8.10.62	London Transport Board	20	Motor Cars
23.4.63	London Transport Board	13	Battery Locos
23.6.64	Mexican Railways	40	Diesel Railcars
30.6.64	Nigerian Railways	33	D.E. Locos 1400hp
19.7.66	Malawi Railways	5	D.E. Locos 1200hp
29.10.66	R.E.N.F.E. (Spain)	10	2 Car Electric Trains
11.2.64	London Transport Board	122	Driving Motor Cars
		122	Trailer Cars
6.6.66	Pakistan Western Railway	29	Electric Locos 3000hp
14.6.66	Trans-Zambesia Railway	7	D.E. Locos 1200hp
30.8.67	London Transport Board	36	Driving Motor Cars
		36	Trailer Cars
1.3.68	London Transport Board	106	Driving Motor Cars
		106	Trailer Cars

APPENDIX 2

Completed Vehicle Output 1945-1978

TERRITORY	LOCOS	COACHES		WAGONS	TOTALS	TERRITORY	LOCOS	COACHES		WAGONS	TOTALS
		Hauled	Powered					Hauled	Powered		
AFRICA						**AUSTRALASIA**					
Angola	-	10	-	635	645	Australia	10	-	-	5566	5576
East Africa	-	192	-	2558	2750	New Zealand	-	-	-	7020	7020
Egypt	-	258	10	1750	2018						
Ghana	-	-	-	304	304	**EUROPE**					
Liberia	-	-	-	159	159	EIRE	94	-	-	-	94
Malawi	10	-	-	-	10	SPAIN	-	10	10	-	20
Mozambique	8	13	-	-	21	UNRRA*	-	-	-	500	500
Nigeria	33	13	4	723	773						
Rhodesia	-	149	-	4378	4527	**U.K.**					
Sierra Leone	-	-	-	40	40	BR and	-	2613	626	37791	41030
South Africa	35	143	267	3614	4059	predecessors					
Zaire	6	12	30	-	48	Glasgow	-	-	26	-	26
						L.T.E.	18	724	2047	-	2789
AMERICA						Private Owners	-	-	-	3637	3637
Central/South						Tyne & Wear	-	-	20	-	20
Mexico	-	-	40	-	40						
Jamaica	-	-	20	-	20	**TOTALS**	309	4,376	3,393	87,373	95,451
Argentina	-	-	-	1450	1450						
Brazil	-	120	190	212	522						
Guyana	-	-	-	54	54						
ASIA											
Borneo	-	-	-	2	2						
Burma	-	-	-	150	150						
Hong Kong	-	23	45	-	68						
India	-	-	58	8368	8426						
Malaysia	40	-	-	410	450						
Pakistan & Bangladesh	55	-	-	6242	6297						
Sri Lanka	-	96	-	40	136						
Turkey	-	-	-	400	400						

*United Nations Relief and Rehabilitation Administration

This 6-coach rake built by Leeds Forge Co. was made for the 5' 6" gauge Great Indian Peninsular Railway's service from Bombay to Delhi.

B.J.R. Yates

The Leeds Forge Co. Ltd.

LEEDS.

Pioneers in the Manufacture of Pressed Steel Underframes and Bogies, and all Steel Railway Wagons.

London Office = CAXTON HOUSE, WESTMINSTER.

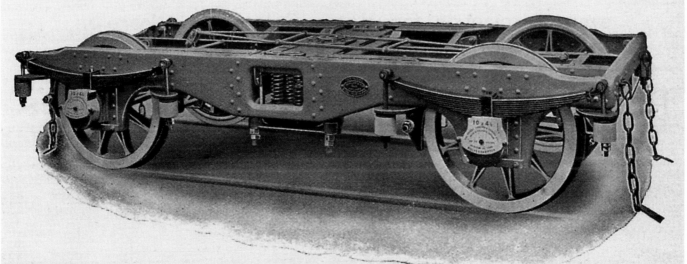

Indian State Railways. (Oudh & Rohilkund Railway). Fox's Pressed Steel Carriage Bogie.

40-Ton Bogie Open Goods Wagon, fitted with Fox's Pressed Steel Underframes and Bogies, and Lane's Patent Corrugated Pressed Steel Doors.

All the vehicles in this appendix were built by The Leeds Forge Co Ltd, who highlighted their 'modern' construction methods in this advertisement. The company was situated at Armley, Leeds with a branch line served by the Midland Railway.

A set of seven 20-ton ballast wagons, numbers 6316 to 6322, built in 1911 for the South Eastern & Chatham Railway is displayed for the photographer in Leeds. The loco is a Midland Railway 0-6-0.

B.J.R. Yates

Two for railways north of the border – Caledonian Railway 15-ton twin wagons, numbers 73169/73170, were built in 1913, while Leeds Forge made the 30-ton bogie swivel wagon in 1914 for the Glasgow & South Western Railway. It featured Fox's pressed steel frameplates.

B.J.R. Yates

These two all-steel cars were constructed for the American-financed London Electric Railway in 1913 and 1914. Trailer Car No.238 had a passenger capacity of 96 (48 seated), while Motor Car No.38 could take 72 passengers (36 seated). Metropolitan Carriage & Wagon built some similar cars for London Electric in 1923. *B.J.R. Yates*

This petrol-electric locomotive, of 600mm gauge, was one of 100 built for the Mechanical Warfare Department of the Ministry of Munitions in 1917. It is awaiting fitting of the motors. The mechanical parts were assembled by Leeds Forge, but the loco carries a Nasmyth Wilson, Manchester, worksplate (1184/1917).   *B.J.R. Yates*

Above: This 10-ton ammonium nitrate wagon went to the National Shell Filling Factory at Chilwell, Nottingham in March 1916.   *B.J.R. Yates*

Below: Another wartime vehicle was this bogie condenser wagon for the Ministry of Munitions in 1917.   *B.J.R. Yates*

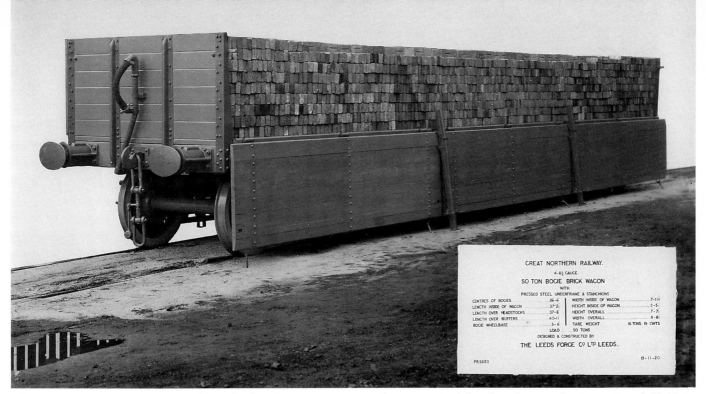

Above: The Great Northern Railway had rail connections to the important brickmaking industry around Fletton, Peterborough, and Leeds Forge designed and built a 50-ton bogie brick wagon for the traffic in 1920. Stacking of the bricks for maximum space utilisation and safe transporting must have been quite an art! *B.J.R. Yates*

Below: Leeds Forge patented this hand operated dump car, capacity 284-cubic feet, which they made in 1928. Its purpose was to enable safe tipping of material somewhat further from the rails than was the case with conventional side tipping wagons, as illustrated here. *B.J.R. Yates*

Above: Leeds Forge built the first all-steel sleeping cars for CIWL in 1922, 'S class' running numbers 2641-2674 and this is one of the batch under construction. When completed, it was painted dark blue which became the standard livery for CIWL's all-steel vehicles. Although a prestigious order, it was not a financial success and led to Leeds Forge being taken over, first by Cammell-Laird and then by Metro-Cammell. *C. Wheeler*

Below: CIWL sleeping car No.2644 in all its external glory, a credit to the skills of Leeds Forge. This first-class car accommodated sixteen passengers. It weighed 54 tons and was a shade under 77' long over the buffers. *C. Wheeler*

Eight standard gauge coaches made, it is believed, in 1925 for Egyptian State Railways, await shipment outside the factory. A notice, on the front coach steps, states they are bound for Alexandria aboard the S.S. Aleppo.

B.J.R. Yates

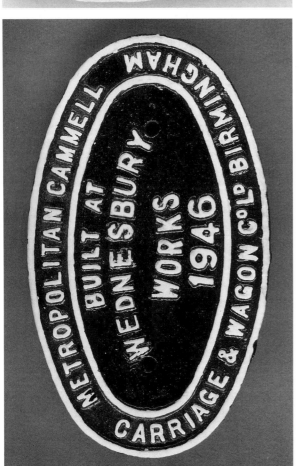

A selection of works plates

BIBLIOGRAPHY

Books

Dudley Docker, The Life and Times of a Trade Warrior
by R Davenport-Hines
(Cambridge University Press, 1984)

L'Egypt et ses Chemins de Fer
by Lionel Wiener
(International Railway Congress Association, 1933)

Eurostar
by Simon Pielow
(Ian Allan, 1997)

History of Trains de Luxe
by George Behrend
(Transport Publishing Company, 1977)

London and Birmingham - A Railway of Consequence
by David Jenkinson
(Capital Transport, 1988)

London's Metropolitan Railway
by Alan A Jackson
(David & Charles, 1986)

Midland Railway Carriages Volume 1
by R.E. Lacy and George Dow
(Wild Swan Publications, 1984)

**Midland & South Western Railway Volume 3
Carriages and Wagons**
by Mike Barnsley
(Wild Swan Publications, 1995)

**Power for the World's Railways -
GEC Traction and its Predecessors**
by R P Bradley
(Oxford Publishing Co, 1993)

Post-Chaise to Wagons Lits
by John Wright
(serialised in The Times, 29 May to 7 June 1907)

Pullman
by Julian Morel
(David & Charles 1983)

The Sentinel 1930-1980
by Anthony R & Joseph L.Thomas,
(Woodpecker 1987)

Steam to Silver
by J Graeme Bruce
(London Transport, 1970)

The Metropolitan Company, 1845-1946
by C O Wallace
(unpublished manuscript in Birmingham Central Library)

Tramcar, Carriage and Wagon Builders of Birmingham
by J H Price
(Nemo Productions, 1982)

Tube Trains under London
by J Graeme Bruce
(London Transport 1968)

Vickers - A History
by J D Scott
(Weidenfeld and Nicholson 1962)

Railway Carriages in the British Isles from 1830 to 1914
by C Hamilton Ellis
(Allen & Unwin 1965)

Periodicals

Bus and Coach

Buses

Engineering

The Engineer

International Railway Journal

Light Railway and Tramway Journal

**Locomotive Magazine and
    Railway Carriage and Wagon Review**

Modern Railways

Modern Transport

Motor Transport

Postal History

Railway Gazette

Railway Magazine

Railway Year Book (Advertisement Pages)

South African Transport

Stock Exchange Year Book

Tramway and Railway World

Metro-Cammell built 175 all-steel containers for the LNER
in 1929 with a 4-ton capacity, also 30 for continental
traffic and 25 for perishable goods.

Also available from Runpast Publishing
10 Kingscote Grove, Cheltenham, Gloucestershire GL51 6JX

THE BIRMINGHAM RAILWAY CARRIAGE & WAGON COMPANY
A CENTURY OF ACHIEVEMENT 1855-1963
by John Hypher, Colin Wheeler, Stephen Wheeler

The Birmingham Railway Carriage and Wagon Company was a significant provider of rolling stock not just for the home market but also exported to an impressive list of world-wide customers.

The company's history is told here for the first time by John Hypher who has written the informative text, while Birmingham-born-and-bred Colin Wheeler, who worked for BRCW, together with his son Stephen, has provided much information and most of the superb quality official works photographs and drawings, showing much detail of interest to modellers of both British and foreign railways. The book also provides a superb memory of a great Birmingham manufacturing company which provided employment for thousands of people for over a hundred years.

In 1902/3 it first built all-steel coaches and in 1910 started construction of Pullman cars, for which the company was rightly famous. 1913 marked the company's first labour dispute which lasted eleven weeks. BRCW played a prominent part in the 1914-18 war effort, manufacturing, among many items; armoured trucks and munitions as well as De Haviland and Handley Page aircraft. Railway work was still carried on, including an eight coach hospital train and 1350 ammunition wagons After the war, business was brisk both at home and overseas for new carriages and wagons, including orders for the famous Compagnie Internationale des Wagons Lits. However competition from continental manufacturers was increasing and making orders harder to get by 1926

The company had diversified into the manufacture of bus and trolleybus bodies and large orders came from London Transport and Birmingham Corporation in the inter-war years, as well as orders for London Underground stock. The 1930s also saw construction of steam and diesel railcars for overseas. Despite this activity, the depression hit the company's output and profitability until 1935 when business began to increase.

During the Second World War production of armaments almost completely filled the order books, with BRCW being one of the foremost manufacturers of tanks, also producing prototypes of several other fighting vehicles. It manufactured the giant all wood Hamilcar heavy transport glider, producing over 400 examples.

After the war, BRCW established itself in the diesel and electric traction market, making locos and railcars for, among others, Australia, New Zealand, Sierra Leone, Eire and Ghana as well as the home railways. It also still had a healthy business in carriages, including Pullmans, and wagons, until lack of orders brought about closure in 1963.

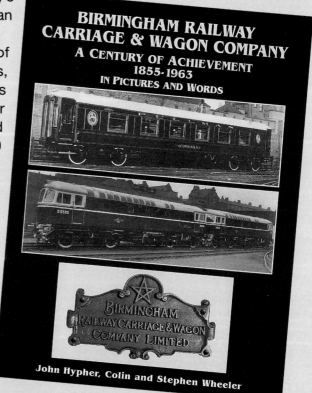

112 pages hardback 273 x 215mm
150 b/w photos, plus line drawings

ISBN 1870754 34 4
Price £14.95